THE EVOLUTION OF HIGH-LEVEL PROGRAMMING LANGUAGES

A Comprehensive Approach to Mastering C, Java, Python, and Beyond for Advanced Software Development

NATHAN WESTWOOD

TABLE OF CONTENTS

languages, C offered a level of abstraction from the machine's hardware, making it more accessible for programmers while still allowing them to have control over system resources.

The C language was designed to be efficient and portable. These qualities made it an immediate success, and over time, C became the basis for many modern programming languages, including C++, Java, and Python. It also influenced the development of operating systems, compilers, and other foundational software.

WHY C STILL MATTERS TODAY:

Despite the rise of many high-level languages, C remains popular for a few key reasons:

- **Efficiency and Control**: C allows direct manipulation of hardware through pointers, which gives programmers more control over the system's resources.
- **Portability**: C code can run on different platforms with little modification, which makes it an ideal language for writing portable software.
- **Foundational Language**: Many programming languages borrow key concepts from C, making it important for developers to understand its syntax and structure.

2.2 The Basics of C Syntax

In this section, we'll break down the fundamental building blocks of the C language: syntax, data types, and structures.

2.2.1 THE STRUCTURE OF A C PROGRAM:

A simple C program consists of several key components:

1. **Preprocessor Directives**: These are instructions to the compiler before the program starts. The most common one is `#include`, which tells the compiler to include a standard or user-defined library. For example, `#include <stdio.h>` includes the standard input/output library.
2. **Main Function**: Every C program must have a `main()` function. It serves as the starting point for program execution.
3. **Statements**: These are the instructions that perform actions, such as printing text or performing calculations.

Here's a basic structure of a C program:

```c
#include <stdio.h>    // Preprocessor directive

int main() {          // Main function
    printf("Hello, World!\n");  // Statement
    return 0;         // Return statement
}
```

- The **#include <stdio.h>** line tells the compiler to include the standard input-output library.
- The **main()** function is the starting point where program execution begins.
- **printf()** is a standard function that outputs text to the console.

2.2.2 VARIABLES AND DATA TYPES:

In C, data is stored in variables, and each variable must be declared with a specific data type. Here are the most common data types in C:

- `int`: Used to store integers (whole numbers).
- `float`: Used to store decimal numbers with single precision.
- `double`: Used to store decimal numbers with double precision.
- `char`: Used to store single characters.

Here's an example of declaring and initializing variables in C:

c

```
int age = 25;       // Declares an integer variable
'age'
float height = 5.9; // Declares a float variable
'height'
char initial = 'J'; // Declares a char variable
'initial'
```

2.2.3 OPERATORS IN C:

C uses operators to perform operations on variables and values. Here are the common categories of operators:

- **Arithmetic Operators**: Used to perform mathematical calculations (+, -, *, /, %).
- **Relational Operators**: Used to compare two values (==, !=, >, <, >=, <=).
- **Logical Operators**: Used to combine multiple conditions (&&, ||, !).

2.3 C Data Structures

C provides several ways to organize and store data, known as **data structures**. The two most commonly used data structures in C are arrays and structures.

2.3.1 ARRAYS IN C:

An array is a collection of elements of the same data type. In C, you declare arrays by specifying the type of elements and the number of elements.

Example:

c

```c
int numbers[5] = {1, 2, 3, 4, 5};
```

This creates an integer array called `numbers` with five elements. You can access individual elements of the array using an index, starting from 0.

2.3.2 STRUCTURES IN C:

A structure (`struct`) is a user-defined data type that groups different types of variables under a single name. This allows you to store more complex data.

Example:

c

```c
struct Person {
    char name[50];
    int age;
    float height;
```

```
};
```

This creates a structure called `Person`, which stores a name (string), age (integer), and height (float). To create and use an instance of a structure, you can do the following:

c

```
struct Person person1;
strcpy(person1.name, "John Doe");
person1.age = 30;
person1.height = 5.9;
```

2.4 Memory Management in C

One of the key reasons C is so powerful is its **direct memory management.** In high-level languages like Python or Java, memory management is automatic (via garbage collection), but in C, you have full control over how memory is allocated and freed.

2.4.1 STATIC MEMORY ALLOCATION:

Static memory allocation occurs at compile time. This means that the size of the memory block must be known ahead of time.

Example:

c

```
int numbers[10]; // Static allocation of 10 integers
```

2.4.2 DYNAMIC MEMORY ALLOCATION:

Dynamic memory allocation allows you to allocate memory at runtime, which is more flexible. You use functions like `malloc()`, `calloc()`, and `free()` to allocate and deallocate memory dynamically.

- **`malloc()`**: Allocates a specified number of bytes of memory.
- **`calloc()`**: Allocates memory for an array of elements and initializes them to zero.
- **`free()`**: Deallocates memory that was previously allocated.

Example:

c

```c
int* ptr = (int*) malloc(5 * sizeof(int)); //
Allocate memory for 5 integers
if (ptr != NULL) {
    // Use the memory
    ptr[0] = 10;
    ptr[1] = 20;
}
free(ptr); // Free the memory
```

Dynamic memory allocation is especially useful when you don't know the amount of memory required at compile time, such as when reading data from files.

2.5 Pointers and Dynamic Memory Allocation

Pointers are one of the most important and powerful features of C. A **pointer** is a variable that stores the memory address of another variable. Understanding pointers is essential for mastering C and programming in general.

2.5.1 DECLARING AND USING POINTERS:

To declare a pointer, you use the * symbol before the variable name. Here's an example:

c

```
int x = 10;
int* ptr = &x; // Pointer stores the address of x
```

In this example, `ptr` is a pointer to an integer, and `&x` gets the address of the variable `x`.

2.5.2 DEREFERENCING POINTERS:

Dereferencing a pointer means accessing the value stored at the memory address it points to. You use the * operator to dereference a pointer:

c

```
printf("%d\n", *ptr); // Dereference ptr to get the
value of x
```

2.5.3 POINTERS AND ARRAYS:

In C, arrays are closely tied to pointers. An array name represents the address of the first element in the array. This means you can use pointers to traverse through arrays.

Example:

```c
int numbers[] = {10, 20, 30};
int* ptr = numbers; // Points to the first element of
the array
printf("%d\n", *(ptr + 1)); // Access the second
element (20)
```

2.6 File Handling and Basic System Operations in C

One of the key features of C is the ability to handle files and interact with the operating system. This is particularly useful for tasks like reading and writing data, logging, or configuring settings.

2.6.1 READING AND WRITING FILES:

C provides functions to work with files, such as `fopen()`, `fclose()`, `fread()`, and `fwrite()`.

Example: Writing to a file:

```c
FILE* file = fopen("example.txt", "w"); // Open a
file for writing
if (file != NULL) {
    fprintf(file, "Hello, World!\n"); // Write to the
file
    fclose(file); // Close the file
}
```

Example: Reading from a file:

c

```c
FILE* file = fopen("example.txt", "r"); // Open a
file for reading
char line[100];
if (file != NULL) {
    fgets(line, sizeof(line), file); // Read a line
from the file
    printf("%s", line); // Print the line
    fclose(file); // Close the file
}
```

2.6.2 SYSTEM OPERATIONS:

C allows interaction with system-level operations such as process control, memory management, and hardware access. The `system()` function is one of the simplest ways to execute system commands from within a C program.

Example:

c

```c
system("mkdir new_directory"); // Executes a shell
command to create a directory
```

2.7 Hands-On Example: Build a Text File Reader and Writer in C

In this section, we will build a simple **text file reader and writer** in C to demonstrate some of the key concepts we've covered so far. This program will:

1. Create a text file and write some data to it.
2. Open the file and read the data back.
3. Display the contents of the file on the console.

```c
c

#include <stdio.h>
#include <stdlib.h>

int main() {
    FILE* file = fopen("sample.txt", "w"); // Open
file for writing
    if (file == NULL) {
        printf("Error opening file for writing.\n");
        return 1;
    }

    fprintf(file, "This is a sample text file.\n");
    fprintf(file, "C programming is powerful!\n");
    fclose(file);

    file = fopen("sample.txt", "r"); // Open file for
reading
    if (file == NULL) {
        printf("Error opening file for reading.\n");
        return 1;
    }

    char line[100];
    while (fgets(line, sizeof(line), file)) {
        printf("%s", line); // Print each line read
from the file
    }

    fclose(file);
    return 0;
}
```

Conclusion

In this chapter, we've laid the groundwork for understanding the C language—its history, syntax, memory management, and pointers. You've learned how to work with C's data types, structures, and file handling, and we've walked through an example of building a simple text file reader and writer. Understanding these fundamentals will give you a strong foundation to move forward with more complex C programming tasks.

Chapter 3: Java – Object-Oriented Programming and Portability

Objective:

This chapter delves into **Java**, exploring its core principles, including **object-oriented programming (OOP)** and **portability**. We will cover key Java concepts like classes, objects, methods, inheritance, and the Java Virtual Machine (JVM), along with exception handling and the powerful collections framework. Java's emphasis on being platform-independent and its continuous relevance in modern software development is also examined.

3.1 Introduction to Java: The Language of Portability

Java was designed with one key goal in mind: to **write once, run anywhere**. This platform-independent philosophy makes Java a popular choice for building cross-platform applications, ranging from mobile apps to enterprise systems. Created in 1991 by **James Gosling** at Sun Microsystems, Java quickly became a game-changer for developers, combining simplicity, performance, and portability.

WHY JAVA?

Java's rise to prominence was fueled by the following characteristics:

- **Object-Oriented Programming (OOP)**: Java brought OOP into the mainstream, making it easier to build reusable, maintainable, and scalable applications.
- **Portability**: Unlike languages that are tightly coupled with specific operating systems or hardware, Java programs can run on any device that supports the **Java Virtual Machine (JVM)**.
- **Security**: Java's security features make it an ideal choice for web-based applications.

By the end of this chapter, you will understand why Java remains relevant in the fast-evolving world of software development.

3.2 Key Java Concepts: Classes, Objects, Methods, and Inheritance

Java is fundamentally an **object-oriented programming (OOP)** language. Understanding the key concepts of OOP is crucial to mastering Java and building modular, scalable software systems.

3.2.1 CLASSES AND OBJECTS

A **class** in Java is a blueprint for creating objects. It defines the properties (also called **fields**) and behaviors (**methods**) that the objects created from it will have. An **object** is an instance of a class.

- **Class Definition**: A class defines the structure of objects, including their data and methods to manipulate that data.

```java
class Car {
    // Fields (properties)
```

```java
    String make;
    String model;
    int year;

    // Constructor (to create an object)
    Car(String make, String model, int year) {
        this.make = make;
        this.model = model;
        this.year = year;
    }

    // Method (behavior)
    void displayCarInfo() {
        System.out.println("Car: " + make + " " +
model + " " + year);
    }
}
```

In the above code:

- The `Car` class has three fields: `make`, `model`, and `year`.
- The constructor is used to initialize the properties when an object of type `Car` is created.
- The `displayCarInfo()` method prints the car's details to the console.

Object Creation: Objects are instances of classes, created using the `new` keyword.

java

```java
Car myCar = new Car("Toyota", "Corolla", 2020); //
Creating an object
myCar.displayCarInfo(); // Calling a method on the
object
```

3.2.2 METHODS

Methods are functions that define the behavior of an object. Methods perform operations on the data stored in fields and can also return a value.

Here's an example:

java

```
class Calculator {
    int add(int a, int b) {
        return a + b;
    }
}
```

- The `add()` method in the `Calculator` class accepts two integers and returns their sum.

3.2.3 INHERITANCE

One of the core principles of OOP is **inheritance**, which allows one class to inherit the properties and methods of another. This promotes reusability and hierarchical classification.

java

```
class Vehicle {
    String brand;

    void start() {
        System.out.println(brand + " is starting");
    }
}

class Car extends Vehicle {
    int wheels;

    void displayCarInfo() {
```

```
        System.out.println("This is a " + brand + "
car with " + wheels + " wheels.");
    }
}
```

In the example above:

- The `Car` class inherits from the `Vehicle` class, meaning it gets the `start()` method and `brand` field.
- The `Car` class adds its own method `displayCarInfo()`.

When creating an object of type `Car`, it can use both the methods from the `Vehicle` class and its own methods:

```
java
```

```
Car myCar = new Car();
myCar.brand = "Toyota";
myCar.wheels = 4;
myCar.start();
myCar.displayCarInfo();
```

3.3 The Java Virtual Machine (JVM) and Portability

3.3.1 WHAT IS THE JVM?

The **Java Virtual Machine (JVM)** is the engine that drives Java's **write once, run anywhere** capability. The JVM enables Java programs to run on any device or operating system that has a JVM implementation.

When you write a Java program, it gets compiled into an intermediate form called **bytecode**. This bytecode is not specific to any machine but is instead designed to be run on the JVM.

1. **Compilation**: Java source code (written in `.java` files) is compiled into bytecode (stored in `.class` files) using the `javac` compiler.
2. **Execution**: The JVM reads the bytecode and translates it into machine code that is specific to the underlying operating system and hardware.

This process ensures that Java programs are **platform-independent**, meaning that once you compile a Java program, you can run it on any machine that has the JVM installed.

3.3.2 THE JVM'S ROLE IN PORTABILITY

Portability is Java's greatest strength. Whether you're developing an application for a Windows machine, a macOS system, or a Linux server, the same Java bytecode can run on all platforms without modification, as long as the JVM is available.

For example, Java applications can be written once and deployed on **Android**, **macOS**, **Windows**, and **Linux** without needing to recompile the code.

3.4 Exception Handling in Java

One of the key features that sets Java apart from older languages is its robust **exception handling** mechanism. Exception handling allows developers to manage runtime errors, ensuring that the program can recover or terminate gracefully without crashing.

3.4.1 WHAT ARE EXCEPTIONS?

An **exception** is an event that disrupts the normal flow of a program. In Java, exceptions are objects that represent errors or unexpected conditions.

- **Checked Exceptions**: These are exceptions that must be explicitly handled by the programmer. Examples include `IOException` and `SQLException`.
- **Unchecked Exceptions**: These are runtime exceptions, such as `NullPointerException`, which do not require explicit handling but should still be managed.

3.4.2 TRY-CATCH BLOCK

Java uses the **try-catch** block to handle exceptions. Code that might throw an exception is placed in the **try** block, while the **catch** block contains code to handle the exception.

java

```
try {
    int result = 10 / 0;
} catch (ArithmeticException e) {
    System.out.println("Error: Division by zero.");
}
```

Here, dividing by zero would normally cause the program to crash. However, the `catch` block catches the `ArithmeticException` and displays a message instead of terminating the program.

3.4.3 THROWING EXCEPTIONS

You can also **throw** your own exceptions using the `throw` keyword. This is useful when you want to enforce certain conditions in your program.

```java
java

if (age < 18) {
    throw new IllegalArgumentException("Age must be
18 or older.");
}
```

3.4.4 THE FINALLY BLOCK

The `finally` block is used for code that needs to run regardless of whether an exception occurred, such as closing a file or releasing resources.

```java
java

try {
    FileReader file = new FileReader("file.txt");
} catch (FileNotFoundException e) {
    System.out.println("File not found.");
} finally {
    System.out.println("Closing resources...");
}
```

3.5 The Collections Framework and Generics

3.5.1 THE COLLECTIONS FRAMEWORK

Java provides a rich set of **collection classes** that make it easier to handle groups of objects. These collections are part of the Java Collections Framework, and include lists, sets, queues, and maps.

- **List**: An ordered collection that allows duplicates, such as `ArrayList` or `LinkedList`.
- **Set**: A collection that does not allow duplicates, such as `HashSet` or `TreeSet`.

- **Map:** A collection that maps keys to values, such as `HashMap` or `TreeMap`.

Example of using a **List**:

```java

import java.util.ArrayList;
import java.util.List;

public class Main {
    public static void main(String[] args) {
        List<String> names = new ArrayList<>();
        names.add("Alice");
        names.add("Bob");
        names.add("Charlie");

        for (String name : names) {
            System.out.println(name);
        }
    }
}
```

3.5.2 GENERICS IN JAVA

Generics in Java allow you to write classes, methods, and interfaces that work with any data type. By using generics, you can enforce type safety without losing the flexibility of using different types of objects.

Example:

```java

class Box<T> {
    private T value;

    public void setValue(T value) {
        this.value = value;
    }
```

```
    public T getValue() {
        return value;
    }
}

Box<Integer> intBox = new Box<>();
intBox.setValue(10);
System.out.println(intBox.getValue());
```

Generics allow `Box` to work with any type, ensuring that only objects
of the specified type can be used.

3.6 Hands-On Example: Building a Basic Java Application Using Objects and Collections

Let's build a simple Java application that demonstrates how to
create objects and use collections. We will create a **Student** class
and use an **ArrayList** to manage a list of students.

```java
import java.util.ArrayList;
import java.util.List;

class Student {
    String name;
    int age;

    Student(String name, int age) {
        this.name = name;
        this.age = age;
    }

    void displayInfo() {
        System.out.println("Student: " + name + ",
Age: " + age);
    }
}
```

```
public class StudentApp {
    public static void main(String[] args) {
        List<Student> students = new ArrayList<>();

        students.add(new Student("Alice", 20));
        students.add(new Student("Bob", 22));
        students.add(new Student("Charlie", 21));

        for (Student student : students) {
            student.displayInfo();
        }
    }
}
```

This application:

- Defines a `Student` class with fields for `name` and `age`.
- Uses an `ArrayList` to store multiple students.
- Iterates over the list to print each student's information.

Conclusion

Java's combination of **object-oriented programming** and **portability** makes it a powerful and versatile language. From classes and inheritance to the JVM and exception handling, Java provides the tools you need to build complex, cross-platform applications. Its collections framework and support for generics further enhance its power, making it a top choice for developers worldwide.

Chapter 4: Python – The Power of Simplicity

Objective:

In this chapter, we will explore Python, one of the most popular programming languages today, known for its simplicity, readability, and versatility. We will cover Python's syntax, the importance of indentation, its ability to integrate with various tools for web development and data analysis, and work with its core data structures. By the end of the chapter, you'll understand why Python has become a go-to language for developers across many fields, including data science, web development, and automation.

4.1 Introduction to Python

Python was created by **Guido van Rossum** in 1980 at the **National Research Institute for Mathematics and Computer Science (CWI)** in the Netherlands. Released in 1991, Python quickly became known for its clear, concise, and readable syntax, which makes it an excellent choice for both beginners and experienced developers. Its design philosophy emphasizes **code readability** and simplicity, which reduces the complexity of programming tasks and enables rapid development.

- **Simplicity**: Python uses clear and easy-to-understand syntax. It looks almost like pseudocode, making it accessible to beginners.
- **Readability**: The use of indentation rather than braces { } to define code blocks enforces a clean, readable code structure.
- **Versatility**: Python can be used for almost anything—web development, data analysis, machine learning, artificial intelligence, automation, and more.
- **Community and Libraries**: Python has a massive community and a rich ecosystem of libraries and frameworks that extend its capabilities.

4.2 Python Syntax and Indentation

Python stands out because of its simple syntax. The way code is structured in Python is intuitive, and it eliminates a lot of unnecessary syntax found in other programming languages, such as semicolons, curly braces, or type declarations. Python is often described as "executable pseudocode," which makes it beginner-friendly.

4.2.1 BASIC SYNTAX

Python syntax is easy to understand. Statements and expressions are written without semicolons at the end of each line (although they can be used in some cases). A typical Python statement might look like this:

```python
print("Hello, World!")
```

- **Whitespace and Indentation**: Python uses **indentation** (whitespace) to define the structure of code blocks, such as loops, conditionals, and functions. This eliminates the need for braces { } and helps keep the code clean.

Example:

```python
if 5 > 3:
    print("5 is greater than 3")
```

In this example, the **indentation** signifies that the `print()` function is inside the `if` block. If the indentation were incorrect, Python would raise an **IndentationError**.

4.2.2 VARIABLES AND DATA TYPES

In Python, variables do not require explicit type declarations. The interpreter automatically infers the data type based on the assigned value.

Example:

```python
x = 10          # Integer
name = "Alice"  # String
price = 9.99    # Float
is_valid = True # Boolean
```

- **Dynamic Typing**: Python uses **dynamic typing**, meaning that variables can change types during runtime. This makes Python very flexible, but requires careful handling of data.

4.3 Functions, Modules, and Libraries

4.3.1 FUNCTIONS IN PYTHON

Functions are one of the key building blocks of Python. A function is defined using the `def` keyword, followed by the function name and parentheses.

python

```python
def greet(name):
    print(f"Hello, {name}!")
```

- The function `greet` accepts a parameter `name` and prints a greeting.
- **Return Values**: Functions can return values using the `return` keyword. This allows you to send a result back from the function to the caller.

python

```python
def add(a, b):
    return a + b

result = add(5, 3)
print(result)   # Outputs: 8
```

4.3.2 MODULES IN PYTHON

Modules are files containing Python code that can be imported into other programs. Modules allow you to organize your code and reuse functionality across different projects.

- **Importing Modules**: You can import built-in modules or your own custom modules.

```python
import math

print(math.sqrt(16))   # Outputs: 4.0
```

- **Creating Your Own Module**: If you save a Python file as `mymodule.py`, you can import it into other programs like so:

```python
import mymodule
```

4.3.3 PYTHON LIBRARIES

Python has a huge ecosystem of **third-party libraries** that provide pre-built functionality for specific tasks. Some of the most popular libraries include:

- **Pandas**: For data manipulation and analysis.
- **Flask and Django**: For web development.
- **NumPy and SciPy**: For scientific and numerical computing.
- **TensorFlow**: For machine learning and AI.

Using libraries reduces the amount of code you need to write and enables you to leverage powerful tools that have been developed by others.

4.4 Python for Web Development and Data Analysis

Python is widely used in both web development and data analysis due to its ease of use and extensive libraries.

4.4.1 PYTHON FOR WEB DEVELOPMENT

Python has several frameworks for web development, with **Flask** and **Django** being the most well-known.

- **Flask**: A lightweight, easy-to-use web framework that is ideal for smaller projects or when you want to build a custom web solution.
- **Django**: A more comprehensive, high-level web framework that comes with built-in features for things like database management, authentication, and more.

Example of creating a simple Flask app:

```python
from flask import Flask

app = Flask(__name__)

@app.route("/")
def hello():
    return "Hello, World!"

if __name__ == "__main__":
    app.run()
```

This script sets up a basic web server that returns "Hello, World!" when accessed.

Python is a powerful tool for **data analysis**. Libraries like **Pandas** and **NumPy** make it easy to manipulate large datasets, perform calculations, and visualize data.

For example, with **Pandas**, you can load and manipulate data from **CSV** files easily:

```python
import pandas as pd

# Load data
data = pd.read_csv("data.csv")

# Perform basic analysis
print(data.head())  # Show the first few rows of the
dataset
```

Python's **Matplotlib** and **Seaborn** libraries also allow for easy **data visualization**, making it a go-to language for data science.

4.5 Working with Data Structures: Lists, Tuples, Dictionaries, and Sets

Python provides several built-in data structures that are both flexible and easy to use.

4.5.1 LISTS

A **list** is an ordered collection of items that can be of different types. Lists are mutable, meaning you can change their contents.

```python
fruits = ["apple", "banana", "cherry"]
fruits.append("orange")  # Add an item to the list
print(fruits[1])  # Access item by index (outputs:
banana)
```

- Lists can store any type of data and support operations like indexing, slicing, and iterating.

4.5.2 TUPLES

A **tuple** is similar to a list but is **immutable**, meaning once created, you cannot modify its contents.

```python
point = (10, 20)
x, y = point  # Tuple unpacking
print(x)  # Outputs: 10
```

- Tuples are useful when you want to store a fixed collection of items.

4.5.3 DICTIONARIES

A **dictionary** is a collection of key-value pairs. Dictionaries are unordered and provide fast access to data using keys.

```python
student = {"name": "Alice", "age": 20, "major":
"Computer Science"}
print(student["name"])  # Outputs: Alice
```

- You can add, remove, and modify dictionary entries easily using keys.

A **set** is an unordered collection of unique elements.

```python
colors = {"red", "blue", "green"}
colors.add("yellow")   # Add an item to the set
print(colors)   # Outputs: {'blue', 'yellow', 'red',
'green'}
```

- Sets are useful when you need to store unique elements and perform operations like union, intersection, and difference.

4.6 Hands-On Example: Build a Python Script That Reads from a CSV File and Processes Data

Now, let's apply what we've learned by creating a Python script that reads data from a **CSV** file and processes it. The script will load the data, clean it, and calculate some basic statistics.

```python
import pandas as pd

# Read CSV file into a DataFrame
data = pd.read_csv("sales_data.csv")

# Display the first few rows
print(data.head())

# Clean the data (remove rows with missing values)
cleaned_data = data.dropna()

# Calculate the total sales
total_sales = cleaned_data["sales"].sum()
print(f"Total Sales: {total_sales}")
```

```
# Group the data by 'region' and calculate the
average sales per region
average_sales_per_region =
cleaned_data.groupby("region")["sales"].mean()
print(average_sales_per_region)
```

<u>EXPLANATION:</u>

- We used **Pandas** to read the CSV file into a **DataFrame**.
- We dropped rows with missing values using `dropna()`.
- We calculated the total sales by summing the sales column.
- We grouped the data by `region` and calculated the average sales for each region.

This simple script demonstrates how to load, clean, and process data with Python. It's just the beginning—Python's data analysis capabilities are vast and powerful.

4.7 Conclusion

Python's simplicity, readability, and versatility make it an ideal language for many types of software development. Whether you're working on web development, data analysis, automation, or scientific computing, Python provides the tools and libraries you need to build efficient and clean solutions.

In this chapter, we've covered the basics of Python syntax, functions, and modules, and we've explored how Python can be used for web development and data analysis. We also worked with Python's core data structures: lists, tuples, dictionaries, and sets, and built a practical script for processing CSV data.

Chapter 5: The Evolution of Languages Beyond C, Java, and Python

Objective:

In this chapter, we will explore the evolution of programming languages that have emerged after C, Java, and Python, focusing on languages like **Rust, Go**, and **Kotlin**. We will also dive into modern programming paradigms, such as **functional programming** and **reactive programming**, and how they've reshaped the way we think about software development. Additionally, we will look at how language interoperability has bridged the gap between different ecosystems and the role of **cloud computing** in shaping the future of programming languages. By the end of this chapter, you'll understand why these languages are gaining popularity and how they are influencing the tech industry.

5.1 New Language Paradigms: Rust, Go, Kotlin

5.1.1 RUST: MEMORY SAFETY WITHOUT GARBAGE COLLECTION

Rust is a systems programming language that focuses on safety, performance, and concurrency. It was created by **Graydon Hoare** at Mozilla in 2010 and has rapidly gained popularity due to its ability to offer memory safety without sacrificing performance.

Rust's unique feature is its **ownership system**, which enforces strict rules on memory management without needing garbage collection. This makes Rust highly efficient for low-level programming tasks, such as operating systems and embedded systems, while preventing common memory errors like **null pointer dereferencing** or **buffer overflows**.

- **Ownership and Borrowing**: In Rust, every value has an owner, and the owner is responsible for cleaning up the value when it's no longer needed. Rust ensures that there's no simultaneous access to a value from multiple places, preventing data races.
- **Concurrency**: Rust's memory safety extends to its **concurrency model**. The language makes it easier to write concurrent code that is both safe and fast by ensuring that data is accessed by only one thread at a time.

Rust's powerful features are particularly appealing for developers working on performance-critical applications, such as game engines, operating systems, and web browsers.

5.1.2 GO: SIMPLICITY AND SCALABILITY FOR CLOUD-NATIVE DEVELOPMENT

Go, often referred to as **Golang**, was developed by **Google** in 2007 and released publicly in 2009. Go was designed to address the challenges that developers face in building scalable, reliable systems, especially in the context of cloud computing.

- **Simplicity and Performance**: Go's syntax is intentionally simple, which makes it easy to learn and use. Unlike many languages that focus on language features, Go emphasizes simplicity and clarity, making it a good fit for team-based development.

- **Concurrency with Goroutines**: One of Go's standout features is its approach to concurrency. With **goroutines**, Go makes it easy to execute concurrent tasks. Goroutines are lightweight, and their management is handled by the Go runtime, which allows developers to write scalable concurrent applications.
- **Garbage Collection**: While Go includes garbage collection, it is designed to be efficient enough for large-scale applications, making Go well-suited for cloud-native applications and microservices.

Go has become the go-to language for many modern web services and cloud computing platforms. Companies like **Google**, **Uber**, **Dropbox**, and **Netflix** use Go to build scalable systems that power their cloud infrastructures.

5.1.3 KOTLIN: MODERN, CONCISE, AND FULLY COMPATIBLE WITH JAVA

Kotlin, created by **JetBrains** in 2011 and officially supported by **Google** for Android development since 2017, is a modern, statically typed language that runs on the **Java Virtual Machine (JVM)**. Kotlin was designed to be fully interoperable with Java while improving on Java's verbosity and limitations.

- **Concise and Expressive Syntax**: Kotlin's syntax is more concise than Java's, reducing boilerplate code and making programs easier to write and maintain. Features like **data classes**, **extension functions**, and **null safety** make Kotlin more developer-friendly.
- **Null Safety**: One of Kotlin's most celebrated features is its built-in **null safety**. In Kotlin, nullability is part of the type system, meaning you can't accidentally assign null to a variable that is not explicitly nullable. This helps eliminate **NullPointerExceptions**, which are common bugs in Java.

- **Functional and Object-Oriented**: Kotlin supports both object-oriented and functional programming paradigms. It's flexible enough to allow you to write functional-style code (with features like higher-order functions and lambdas) while still being object-oriented at its core.

Kotlin has gained a lot of traction in the Android development community, thanks to its clear, readable syntax and interoperability with Java. Many Android developers now prefer Kotlin over Java due to its conciseness and modern features.

5.2 The Rise of Functional and Reactive Programming

5.2.1 FUNCTIONAL PROGRAMMING: A SHIFT TOWARD IMMUTABILITY AND PURITY

Functional programming (FP) is a paradigm that treats computation as the evaluation of mathematical functions and avoids changing state or mutable data. While functional programming concepts have been around for decades, they've gained significant traction in modern languages like **Haskell**, **Scala**, **JavaScript**, and even **Java** (through lambdas and the Streams API).

- **Immutability:** In FP, data is immutable by default, meaning once a value is assigned to a variable, it cannot be changed. This helps reduce side effects, making the code easier to reason about and test.
- **First-Class Functions**: Functions are treated as first-class citizens in FP, meaning they can be passed as arguments to other functions, returned as values, and assigned to variables.

- **Pure Functions**: A pure function is one that always produces the same output given the same input and has no side effects. This makes pure functions predictable and easy to test.

Languages like **Haskell, Scala**, and **Elixir** are purely functional, while others like **JavaScript**, **Python**, and **Java** incorporate functional programming features.

5.2.2 REACTIVE PROGRAMMING: HANDLING ASYNCHRONOUS DATA STREAMS

Reactive programming is a paradigm for handling asynchronous data streams and the propagation of changes. It's become especially popular with the rise of real-time applications, such as chat apps, live updates, and dashboards.

- **Observables and Streams**: In reactive programming, data is treated as a stream that can be observed and reacted to. A stream of data could represent user inputs, sensor readings, or messages from a server.
- **Backpressure**: One of the challenges of reactive programming is dealing with situations where data is flowing too quickly for the system to process. **Backpressure** mechanisms are used to control the flow of data to prevent overload.

ReactiveX (Reactive Extensions) is a popular library for reactive programming, and it's available in many programming languages, including JavaScript, Java, and Python.

5.3 Language Interoperability: Bridging Different Ecosystems

One of the challenges in modern software development is **language interoperability**, or the ability for different programming languages to work together. As software ecosystems become more complex and diverse, being able to use different languages in the same system becomes increasingly important.

5.3.1 JAVASCRIPT WITH TYPESCRIPT

TypeScript is a statically typed superset of **JavaScript** that compiles to plain JavaScript. While JavaScript is a flexible and widely-used language, it lacks built-in support for type checking, which can lead to errors in large applications.

TypeScript solves this by introducing type annotations and type checking. It allows developers to write cleaner, safer code and provides an easier migration path for existing JavaScript projects.

```typescript
let message: string = "Hello, World!";
message = 10; // This will cause an error because
message is expected to be a string.
```

The compatibility of TypeScript with JavaScript allows developers to use TypeScript gradually in existing JavaScript codebases, leading to fewer bugs and more maintainable code.

5.3.2 PYTHON AND C/C++ INTEGRATION

Python is a high-level interpreted language, and while it's easy to use, it's not the fastest language for performance-critical applications. To address this, Python allows integration with **C** and

C++, which are much faster languages for tasks like numerical computation, graphics, and hardware control.

Using tools like **Cython** or **ctypes**, you can call C functions directly from Python, enabling you to write performance-critical parts of your program in C while keeping the ease of use and flexibility of Python for the rest of the code.

5.4 The Impact of Cloud Computing on Programming Languages

Cloud computing has dramatically transformed the way applications are developed, deployed, and scaled. It has created new demands for programming languages and frameworks, driving the evolution of modern languages.

5.4.1 SCALABILITY AND DISTRIBUTED SYSTEMS

Languages like **Go** and **Rust** have gained popularity in cloud computing because of their **concurrency models** and ability to manage large-scale, distributed systems. These languages excel at building **microservices**, which are small, independently deployable services that can scale and be updated independently in a cloud environment.

- **Go** is particularly suited for cloud-native development due to its built-in concurrency model (goroutines) and ease of deployment.
- **Rust** is favored for tasks that require both high performance and memory safety, such as network programming and system-level development.

The rise of **serverless computing** and **edge computing** has introduced new ways of building and deploying applications. In serverless computing, developers focus on writing functions that are executed in response to events, and cloud providers handle the scaling and infrastructure.

Languages like **JavaScript, Go,** and **Python** are commonly used in serverless applications because of their speed and ease of integration with cloud platforms like **AWS Lambda, Google Cloud Functions,** and **Azure Functions**.

5.5 Hands-On Example: Write a "To-Do" App in Kotlin Using Its Object-Oriented Features

Now, let's apply some of what we've learned by writing a basic **"To-Do" app** in **Kotlin**. This app will demonstrate Kotlin's object-oriented features, including classes, objects, and methods.

```kotlin
// Define a ToDoItem class to represent each task
data class ToDoItem(val task: String, var
isCompleted: Boolean = false)

// Define a ToDoList class to manage a list of tasks
class ToDoList {
    private val tasks = mutableListOf<ToDoItem>()

    fun addTask(task: String) {
        tasks.add(ToDoItem(task))
    }

    fun markTaskAsCompleted(index: Int) {
```

```kotlin
        if (index in tasks.indices) {
            tasks[index].isCompleted = true
        }
    }

    fun showTasks() {
        for ((index, task) in tasks.withIndex()) {
            println("${index + 1}. ${task.task} -
${if (task.isCompleted) "Completed" else "Pending"}")
        }
    }
}

fun main() {
    val myToDoList = ToDoList()
    myToDoList.addTask("Buy groceries")
    myToDoList.addTask("Finish homework")
    myToDoList.showTasks()

    myToDoList.markTaskAsCompleted(0)
    println("\nAfter marking the first task as
completed:")
    myToDoList.showTasks()
}
```

EXPLANATION:

- **ToDoItem Class**: Represents a single task with properties `task` (the task description) and `isCompleted` (indicating whether the task is done).
- **ToDoList Class**: Manages a list of tasks. It has methods to add tasks, mark them as completed, and display the task list.
- The `main()` function demonstrates creating a `ToDoList` object, adding tasks, and updating their status.

5.6 Conclusion

The evolution of programming languages beyond C, Java, and Python has brought new languages like **Rust**, **Go**, and **Kotlin** into the spotlight. These languages address specific challenges in modern software development, such as memory safety, concurrency, and mobile app development. Along with the rise of functional and reactive programming, these new languages provide developers with the tools they need to build robust, scalable, and high-performance applications.

The emergence of cloud computing has further influenced language design, emphasizing the need for languages that support distributed systems, serverless architectures, and edge computing.

As we continue to see new language trends and paradigms, it's important to keep learning and adapting to these changes. With **Kotlin**, **Go**, and **Rust** leading the charge, the future of programming looks more efficient, versatile, and powerful than ever before.

Chapter 6: Memory Management in High-Level Languages

Objective:

In this chapter, we will explore how memory is managed in high-level programming languages, including Java, Python, and C. We will delve into the different ways these languages handle memory allocation and deallocation, with a special focus on **garbage collection** in Java and Python and **manual memory management** in C. The chapter will explain **stack vs. heap memory**, **memory leaks**, and how to prevent them. By the end of the chapter, you will understand how memory management affects your programs' performance and how to write more efficient and reliable code.

6.1 Introduction to Memory Management

Memory management is a fundamental concept in programming that deals with how memory is allocated and freed during the execution of a program. Different programming languages handle memory management in different ways, from **automatic garbage collection** to **manual memory allocation**.

Memory is a **limited resource** that your program uses to store data and instructions. How well you manage memory can significantly impact your program's performance and reliability. Poor memory

management can lead to issues such as **memory leaks,
segmentation faults**, and **program crashes**.

6.2 Stack vs. Heap Memory

To understand memory management, we first need to differentiate
between **stack memory** and **heap memory**, the two primary regions
of memory used by programs.

6.2.1 STACK MEMORY

The **stack** is a region of memory used for **automatic memory
allocation**. When a function is called, the local variables are pushed
onto the stack. When the function exits, the local variables are
popped off the stack, and the memory is automatically reclaimed.

- **Scope and Lifetime**: Variables on the stack are only
  accessible within the scope of the function in which they are
  defined. Once the function finishes execution, the memory is
  freed.
- **Efficiency**: Stack memory is much faster than heap memory
  because memory is allocated and deallocated in a last-in,
  first-out (LIFO) order. This makes stack memory more
  efficient.
- **Limitations**: The stack is limited in size, and trying to
  allocate too much memory on the stack can cause a **stack
  overflow**.

Example:

c

```
void function() {
```

```
    int localVar = 10;   // Allocated on the stack
    printf("%d", localVar);   // Local variable used
here
}   // localVar is automatically deallocated when the
function ends
```

In the above example, the `localVar` is stored on the stack, and once the `function()` finishes, the memory is automatically freed.

6.2.2 HEAP MEMORY

The **heap** is a region of memory used for **dynamic memory allocation**. Unlike the stack, memory on the heap is allocated manually by the programmer, and the programmer is also responsible for deallocating it.

- **Scope and Lifetime**: Variables in the heap can be accessed globally, and their lifetime is controlled manually by the programmer.
- **Efficiency**: Memory allocation on the heap is slower than the stack because it involves more complex management of memory blocks.
- **Flexibility**: The heap allows for the allocation of large data structures or objects whose size might not be known at compile time.
- **Memory Leaks**: A major downside to heap memory is the potential for **memory leaks**, which occur when memory is allocated but never deallocated.

Example:

c

```
void function() {
    int* ptr = (int*)malloc(sizeof(int));   //
Allocated on the heap
```

```
    *ptr = 10;   // Assign value to the allocated
memory
    free(ptr);   // Manually deallocate memory
}   // The memory pointed by ptr is freed manually
```

In this example, `malloc()` is used to allocate memory on the heap, and `free()` is used to deallocate it. If `free()` were omitted, the program would suffer from a **memory leak**.

6.3 Memory Leaks and Avoiding Them

A **memory leak** occurs when a program allocates memory but fails to deallocate it when it's no longer needed. Over time, memory leaks can lead to **increased memory usage** and **program crashes**, especially in long-running applications.

6.3.1 CAUSES OF MEMORY LEAKS

- **Not freeing heap memory**: In languages like C and C++, if you allocate memory with `malloc()` or `new`, you need to explicitly free it with `free()` or `delete`. If this step is missed, memory will not be reclaimed.
- **Losing references to dynamically allocated memory**: If a pointer or reference to dynamically allocated memory is overwritten or goes out of scope without freeing the memory, it becomes **orphaned** and cannot be reclaimed, leading to a leak.

6.3.2 DETECTING AND PREVENTING MEMORY LEAKS

- **Use of memory management tools**: Tools like **Valgrind** for C and C++ can help detect memory leaks by analyzing the program's memory usage.

- **Automatic memory management**: Languages like Java and Python use **garbage collection**, which automatically detects and frees memory that is no longer in use.
- **Adopting smart pointers in C++**: Smart pointers, such as `std::unique_ptr` and `std::shared_ptr`, automatically manage memory allocation and deallocation, making it easier to avoid memory leaks.

6.4 The Role of Garbage Collection in Java and Python

Garbage collection (GC) is a process used by high-level programming languages like **Java** and **Python** to **automatically reclaim memory** that is no longer needed by the program. The primary advantage of GC is that it reduces the risk of memory leaks and removes the burden of manual memory management from developers.

6.4.1 HOW GARBAGE COLLECTION WORKS

- **Mark-and-Sweep Algorithm**: One of the most common garbage collection algorithms is **mark-and-sweep**. The GC first **marks** all the objects that are still in use by the program. It then **sweeps** through the heap and reclaims memory from objects that are no longer referenced.
- **Generational Garbage Collection**: Modern garbage collectors use a **generational approach**, which divides the heap into different generations (young, old, and permanent). Objects that survive longer are promoted to older generations, and garbage collection is performed more frequently on younger objects.

6.4.2 GARBAGE COLLECTION IN JAVA

In Java, the JVM's garbage collector automatically manages memory. The most common garbage collection algorithm used in Java is the **Garbage-First (G1) Garbage Collector**, which aims to achieve low-latency and high-throughput collection.

Example in Java:

```java
public class Main {
    public static void main(String[] args) {
        String str1 = new String("Hello");
        String str2 = new String("World");
        str1 = null;  // After this, str1 is no
longer reachable, and the memory can be reclaimed
        System.gc();  // Request garbage collection
(not guaranteed to run immediately)
    }
}
```

In this example, the string str1 is no longer referenced after it is set to null, and the JVM's garbage collector can reclaim the memory when it runs.

6.4.3 GARBAGE COLLECTION IN PYTHON

Python's garbage collection works similarly to Java's but with a focus on **reference counting** and **cyclic garbage collection**. In Python, every object has a reference count, and when the count drops to zero, the memory is reclaimed. Python also has a cyclic garbage collector to handle reference cycles (e.g., two objects referencing each other).

Example in Python:

```python
python

import gc

class Person:
    def __init__(self, name):
        self.name = name

# Creating an object and making it eligible for
garbage collection
person1 = Person("Alice")
person1 = None   # person1 is now unreferenced

gc.collect()   # Explicitly trigger garbage collection
```

In this example, setting `person1` to `None` makes it eligible for garbage collection. Python's garbage collector will eventually reclaim the memory.

6.5 Manual Memory Management in C with `malloc()` and `free()`

While languages like Java and Python handle memory management automatically, **C** requires developers to manually allocate and deallocate memory using `malloc()`, `calloc()`, `free()`, and similar functions. This gives developers more control over memory but also introduces the risk of **memory leaks** and **segmentation faults**.

6.5.1 MALLOC () AND FREE () IN C

- **`malloc()`**: Allocates a block of memory of a specified size. If the allocation is successful, it returns a pointer to the allocated memory.
- **`free()`**: Frees a block of memory that was previously allocated with `malloc()`.

Example:

c

```c
#include <stdio.h>
#include <stdlib.h>

int main() {
    int* ptr = (int*)malloc(sizeof(int));   // Allocates memory for an integer
    if (ptr == NULL) {
        printf("Memory allocation failed.\n");
        return 1;
    }

    *ptr = 100;   // Assign a value to the allocated memory
    printf("Value: %d\n", *ptr);   // Print the value

    free(ptr);   // Free the allocated memory
    return 0;
}
```

In this example, we allocate memory for an integer using `malloc()`, assign a value to it, print the value, and then free the memory using `free()`.

6.5.2 COMMON PITFALLS AND MEMORY LEAKS IN C

One of the most common issues with manual memory management is **memory leaks**—failing to free memory after it's no longer needed. Here's an example of a memory leak in C:

c

```c
#include <stdio.h>
#include <stdlib.h>

void createMemoryLeak() {
```

```c
    int* ptr = (int*)malloc(sizeof(int));   // Memory
allocated
    *ptr = 10;
    // Memory is not freed, causing a memory leak
}

int main() {
    createMemoryLeak();
    return 0;
}
```

In the above example, the allocated memory is never freed, causing a memory leak. To fix this, we need to ensure `free()` is called after the memory is no longer needed.

6.6 Hands-On Example: Create a C Program to Demonstrate Memory Leaks and Then Fix It Using Proper Memory Management Techniques

Let's write a simple C program that demonstrates a **memory leak** and then fix it by properly managing memory.

c

```c
#include <stdio.h>
#include <stdlib.h>

void createMemoryLeak() {
    int* ptr = (int*)malloc(sizeof(int));   // Memory
allocated
    if (ptr == NULL) {
        printf("Memory allocation failed.\n");
        return;
    }
    *ptr = 100;   // Assign a value
    // Memory is not freed, causing a memory leak
}
```

```c
void fixMemoryLeak() {
    int* ptr = (int*)malloc(sizeof(int));   // Memory
allocated
    if (ptr == NULL) {
        printf("Memory allocation failed.\n");
        return;
    }
    *ptr = 100;   // Assign a value
    printf("Value: %d\n", *ptr);
    free(ptr);   // Properly free the memory
}

int main() {
    createMemoryLeak();   // Call the function that
causes a memory leak
    printf("Fixed memory leak version:\n");
    fixMemoryLeak();   // Call the function that fixes
the leak
    return 0;
}
```

In this example:

- The `createMemoryLeak()` function demonstrates a memory leak by allocating memory but never freeing it.
- The `fixMemoryLeak()` function correctly frees the allocated memory using `free()`.

6.7 Conclusion

Memory management is a critical aspect of software development. In languages like Java and Python, **garbage collection** automates memory management, reducing the burden on developers. However, in lower-level languages like C, developers must manually allocate and free memory, which gives more control but also introduces the risk of memory leaks and segmentation faults.

By understanding how memory management works in different languages, you can write more efficient, reliable, and performant code. Whether using **automatic garbage collection** or **manual memory management**, it's essential to be mindful of how memory is allocated, used, and freed in your programs.

Chapter 7: From Procedural to Object-Oriented Programming

Objective:

This chapter will explain the shift from **procedural programming** to **object-oriented programming (OOP)**, highlighting the advantages of OOP in creating scalable, maintainable, and modular applications. We will explore the key principles of OOP— **Encapsulation**, **Inheritance**, **Polymorphism**, and **Abstraction**— and provide real-world examples of where and how these principles are applied. By the end of this chapter, you'll have a clear understanding of the core differences between procedural and object-oriented programming and how OOP has revolutionized software development.

7.1 Introduction to Programming Paradigms

Before diving into the specifics of object-oriented programming, it's important to understand the two major programming paradigms: **procedural programming** and **object-oriented programming (OOP)**. These paradigms represent different approaches to organizing and managing code.

7.1.1 PROCEDURAL PROGRAMMING

Procedural programming is based on the concept of the **procedure** or **function**, which is a sequence of instructions that operates on data. In procedural programming, code is typically organized into functions, and these functions manipulate data structures such as arrays or lists.

- **Key Characteristics of Procedural Programming**:
  - Functions or procedures are the primary building blocks.
  - The focus is on **what** the program should do.
  - Data and functions are separate entities.
  - Execution follows a top-down approach, where instructions are executed in the order they are written.

Example: A simple procedural program in **C** that calculates the area of a rectangle might look like this:

c

```c
#include <stdio.h>

float calculateArea(float length, float width) {
    return length * width;
}

int main() {
    float length = 5.0;
    float width = 3.0;
    printf("Area: %.2f\n", calculateArea(length,
width));
    return 0;
}
```

In this procedural program, we have a **function** (calculateArea) that calculates the area based on the **data** (length and width). The function is a separate entity from the data.

Object-oriented programming, on the other hand, organizes code around **objects**. These objects are instances of **classes**, and they encapsulate both **data** (attributes) and **functions** (methods). The focus of OOP is not only on what the program should do but also on **how** the program should structure its behavior and data.

- **Key Characteristics of OOP**:
    - **Classes and Objects**: Classes are blueprints for creating objects, which are instances of these classes.
    - **Encapsulation**: Data and methods are bundled together inside objects.
    - **Inheritance**: Classes can inherit properties and behaviors from other classes.
    - **Polymorphism**: Methods in different classes can have the same name but behave differently depending on the class.
    - **Abstraction**: The complexity of an object is hidden, and only relevant details are exposed to the user.

In contrast to procedural programming, OOP emphasizes creating modular, reusable components that can be easily extended or modified.

7.2 Key Principles of OOP

Let's dive deeper into the **four fundamental principles of object-oriented programming**:

7.2.1 ENCAPSULATION

Encapsulation is the process of bundling data (attributes) and methods (functions) that operate on the data within a single unit, called a **class**. Encapsulation helps protect data by restricting direct access to an object's attributes and providing access through well-defined methods (getters and setters).

- **Why is Encapsulation Important?:**
    - It **protects data**: By controlling access to data, you can prevent unintended interference or modification.
    - It **reduces complexity**: By hiding the internal workings of a class, users only interact with the exposed methods, reducing the complexity of interacting with the class.
    - It **improves maintainability**: Changes made to the internal structure of a class do not affect the external code that uses the class.

Example: In Java, we can encapsulate the attributes of a Car class using **private fields** and provide access to them via **public methods** (getters and setters):

```java
public class Car {
    private String make;
    private String model;
    private int year;

    public Car(String make, String model, int year) {
        this.make = make;
        this.model = model;
        this.year = year;
    }

    // Getter method
    public String getMake() {
        return make;
```

```
        }

        // Setter method
        public void setMake(String make) {
            this.make = make;
        }

        // Method to display car details
        public void displayDetails() {
            System.out.println("Car: " + make + " " +
model + " " + year);
        }
    }
```

In the above example, `make`, `model`, and `year` are encapsulated within the `Car` class. The `getMake()` and `setMake()` methods provide controlled access to the `make` attribute.

7.2.2 INHERITANCE

Inheritance allows one class (the subclass or child class) to inherit attributes and methods from another class (the superclass or parent class). This enables **code reuse** and establishes a relationship between different classes.

- **Why is Inheritance Important?:**
    - It **promotes reusability**: Common functionality can be written once in a parent class and shared by many child classes.
    - It **models real-world relationships**: Inheritance is a natural way to model relationships between different entities, like a `Dog` class inheriting from an `Animal` class.
    - It **enhances maintainability**: Changes made to the parent class automatically propagate to the child classes.

Example: In Java, a `Dog` class can inherit from a more general `Animal` class:

java

```java
class Animal {
    public void sound() {
        System.out.println("Animal makes a sound");
    }
}

class Dog extends Animal {
    public void sound() {
        System.out.println("Dog barks");
    }
}

public class Main {
    public static void main(String[] args) {
        Animal animal = new Animal();
        animal.sound();   // Outputs: Animal makes a sound

        Dog dog = new Dog();
        dog.sound();   // Outputs: Dog barks
    }
}
```

Here, `Dog` is a subclass of `Animal`, and it **overrides** the `sound()` method. This illustrates the concept of inheritance and method overriding.

7.2.3 POLYMORPHISM

Polymorphism allows objects of different classes to be treated as objects of a common superclass. The most common use of polymorphism is when a subclass overrides a method from the superclass. This allows the method to behave differently depending on the object calling it.

- **Why is Polymorphism Important?**:
    - It **increases flexibility**: You can write more generic code that works with objects of different types.
    - It **reduces redundancy**: You can use the same method name for different implementations, reducing the need for multiple method names.
    - It **simplifies code**: Polymorphism allows you to handle objects of different types in a unified way.

Example: In Java, polymorphism allows different classes to provide their own implementation of a method defined in a common interface or superclass:

```java
class Animal {
    public void sound() {
        System.out.println("Animal makes a sound");
    }
}

class Dog extends Animal {
    public void sound() {
        System.out.println("Dog barks");
    }
}

class Cat extends Animal {
    public void sound() {
        System.out.println("Cat meows");
    }
}

public class Main {
    public static void main(String[] args) {
        Animal animal = new Animal();
        Animal dog = new Dog();
```

```
        Animal cat = new Cat();

        animal.sound();   // Outputs: Animal makes a
sound
        dog.sound();      // Outputs: Dog barks
        cat.sound();      // Outputs: Cat meows
    }
}
```

In this example, polymorphism allows the `sound()` method to behave differently depending on whether it's called on an `Animal`, `Dog`, or `Cat` object.

7.2.4 ABSTRACTION

Abstraction involves hiding the complexity of a system and exposing only the necessary parts. It is the process of defining **abstract classes** and **interfaces** that provide the basic structure for other classes to implement.

- **Why is Abstraction Important?**:
    - It **simplifies interfaces**: By exposing only relevant details, abstraction hides unnecessary complexity.
    - It **improves flexibility**: You can define abstract classes or interfaces that can be implemented by multiple classes.
    - It **promotes loose coupling**: Abstraction helps to decouple components by focusing on high-level interactions rather than implementation details.

Example: In Java, abstraction can be achieved using abstract classes and interfaces:

```java
java
```

```java
abstract class Animal {
    public abstract void sound();   // Abstract method
}

class Dog extends Animal {
    public void sound() {
        System.out.println("Dog barks");
    }
}

class Cat extends Animal {
    public void sound() {
        System.out.println("Cat meows");
    }
}

public class Main {
    public static void main(String[] args) {
        Animal dog = new Dog();
        dog.sound();   // Outputs: Dog barks

        Animal cat = new Cat();
        cat.sound();   // Outputs: Cat meows
    }
}
```

In this example, `Animal` is an **abstract class** with an abstract
method `sound()`, which is implemented by the subclasses `Dog` and
`Cat`.

7.3 Comparing Procedural and Object-Oriented Programming

7.3.1 PROCEDURAL PROGRAMMING: A TOP-DOWN APPROACH

In procedural programming, the program is structured around
functions or procedures that operate on data. The primary focus is
on **functions** and the **sequential flow** of operations.

- **Data and Functions**: Data and functions are separate entities. Data is manipulated by functions, and the flow of control is generally linear.
- **Modularity**: In procedural programming, modularity is achieved by breaking down the program into smaller functions. However, functions often operate on global data, which can make the code harder to manage in larger systems.
- **Scalability**: While procedural programming works well for small, simple programs, it can become difficult to manage as the complexity of the system increases.

7.3.2 OBJECT-ORIENTED PROGRAMMING: A BOTTOM-UP APPROACH

OOP, on the other hand, structures the program around **objects** that contain both data and methods. This approach focuses on modeling real-world entities as objects that interact with each other.

- **Encapsulation and Data Hiding**: OOP promotes the concept of **encapsulation**, where data and methods are bundled together, and access to data is controlled through methods.
- **Code Reusability and Extensibility**: OOP allows for code reuse through **inheritance** and **polymorphism**, making it easier to extend the system by adding new classes without affecting the existing codebase.
- **Maintainability**: OOP's modular structure, along with its support for abstraction and inheritance, makes it easier to manage and maintain large applications.

7.4 Hands-On Example: Convert a Procedural C Program into an Object-Oriented Java Program

Let's take a simple **procedural C program** that calculates the area of a rectangle and convert it into an **object-oriented Java program**.

PROCEDURAL C PROGRAM

```c
#include <stdio.h>

float calculateArea(float length, float width) {
    return length * width;
}

int main() {
    float length = 5.0;
    float width = 3.0;
    printf("Area: %.2f\n", calculateArea(length, width));
    return 0;
}
```

OBJECT-ORIENTED JAVA PROGRAM

```java
public class Rectangle {
    private float length;
    private float width;

    // Constructor to initialize the rectangle
    public Rectangle(float length, float width) {
        this.length = length;
        this.width = width;
    }

    // Method to calculate the area
    public float calculateArea() {
        return length * width;
```

```
    }

    // Method to display the area
    public void displayArea() {
        System.out.println("Area: " +
calculateArea());
    }

    public static void main(String[] args) {
        Rectangle rectangle = new Rectangle(5.0f,
3.0f);
        rectangle.displayArea();
    }
}
```

In the Java version:

- We defined a **Rectangle** class that encapsulates the properties (length and width) and methods (calculateArea and displayArea).
- The **main()** method creates an instance of Rectangle and calculates the area using the object's method.

7.5 Conclusion

The shift from procedural programming to object-oriented programming represents a significant evolution in how we structure and manage code. While procedural programming focuses on functions and a linear flow of control, OOP introduces a more modular and reusable approach through **encapsulation, inheritance, polymorphism**, and **abstraction**.

OOP has become the dominant paradigm in modern software development, providing numerous advantages such as scalability, maintainability, and code reuse. By understanding the principles of

OOP and comparing it to procedural programming, developers can choose the best approach for their projects.

Chapter 8: Concurrency and Parallelism in High-Level Languages

Objective:

This chapter explores the concepts of **concurrency** and **parallelism**, which are crucial for building efficient and high-performance applications. While these terms are often used interchangeably, they have distinct meanings and implications in software development. We'll focus on how high-level programming languages like **C**, **Java**, and **Python** manage concurrent execution, and we'll look at the challenges of managing multiple threads and processes in these languages. The chapter will discuss how **thread synchronization** works, the **Global Interpreter Lock (GIL)** in Python, and concurrency utilities in Java like the **Executor framework**. By the end of this chapter, you'll understand the fundamental principles behind concurrent and parallel programming and how to implement these concepts in real-world applications.

8.1 Introduction to Concurrency and Parallelism

8.1.1 WHAT IS CONCURRENCY?

Concurrency refers to the ability of a program to handle multiple tasks at the same time. This doesn't necessarily mean that the tasks are being executed simultaneously; instead, it means that the program is able to manage multiple tasks and make progress on each one, often by switching between them rapidly. Concurrency is particularly useful when a program needs to perform several operations that are independent of each other, such as handling user input while performing background tasks.

For example, consider a web server that needs to handle multiple client requests. Even though it may not be able to serve them all at once, it can process them concurrently by rapidly switching between tasks, providing the illusion that everything is happening simultaneously.

8.1.2 WHAT IS PARALLELISM?

Parallelism, on the other hand, refers to executing multiple tasks at exactly the same time. This typically requires multiple processors or cores, where each core executes a separate task simultaneously. Parallelism is particularly useful for tasks that are computationally intensive and can be broken down into smaller, independent subtasks that can be executed simultaneously.

An example of parallelism would be running multiple simulations in a scientific application where each simulation is independent and can run on a different processor core, greatly speeding up the overall process.

8.1.3 THE RELATIONSHIP BETWEEN CONCURRENCY AND PARALLELISM

Concurrency and parallelism are closely related but distinct concepts:

- **Concurrency** is about managing multiple tasks at the same time (which may or may not be executed simultaneously).
- **Parallelism** is about executing multiple tasks simultaneously on different processors or cores.

Concurrency can be implemented without parallelism (using a single-core processor), while parallelism inherently involves concurrency, as multiple tasks are being executed at the same time.

8.2 Threads and Processes in C, Java, and Python

8.2.1 THREADS IN C

In **C**, threads are typically created using **POSIX threads** (or **pthreads**) on Unix-like systems. A thread is a lightweight process that shares the same memory space as the main program. Threads are useful for executing concurrent tasks within the same program.

- **Creating Threads**: Threads are created using the `pthread_create()` function.
- **Synchronization**: Because threads share memory, synchronization mechanisms (such as **mutexes** and **condition variables**) are necessary to avoid race conditions.

Example of creating a simple thread in C using `pthread`:

c

```
#include <stdio.h>
#include <pthread.h>

void* printHello(void* arg) {
    printf("Hello from thread\n");
```

```
    return NULL;
}

int main() {
    pthread_t thread;
    pthread_create(&thread, NULL, printHello, NULL);
    pthread_join(thread, NULL);  // Wait for the
thread to finish
    printf("Hello from main\n");
    return 0;
}
```

This program creates a new thread that prints a message, and the main thread waits for it to complete before printing its own message.

8.2.2 THREADS IN JAVA

In **Java**, threads are part of the core API and are managed through the `Thread` class or the `Executor` framework. Java provides a higher-level abstraction for creating and managing threads compared to C.

- **Creating Threads**: A thread can be created by either extending the `Thread` class or implementing the `Runnable` interface.
- **Synchronization**: Java provides synchronization mechanisms like `synchronized` blocks and `ReentrantLock` to handle shared data among threads.

Example of creating a thread in Java by implementing `Runnable`:

```java
class MyThread implements Runnable {
    public void run() {
        System.out.println("Hello from thread");
    }
}
```

```
public class Main {
    public static void main(String[] args) {
        Thread thread = new Thread(new MyThread());
        thread.start();
        System.out.println("Hello from main");
    }
}
```

8.2.3 THREADS IN PYTHON

In **Python,** the `threading` module provides a way to create and manage threads. However, Python's **Global Interpreter Lock (GIL)** restricts the execution of multiple threads in a single process to only one thread at a time for CPU-bound tasks. This means that while threads can be used for I/O-bound tasks (such as reading files or making network requests), they may not offer significant performance improvements for CPU-bound tasks.

- **Creating Threads**: Threads are created by instantiating the `Thread` class and calling `start()`.
- **Synchronization**: Python provides synchronization tools like `Lock`, `RLock`, and `Condition`.

Example of creating a thread in Python:

```python
python

import threading

def print_hello():
    print("Hello from thread")

# Create and start the thread
thread = threading.Thread(target=print_hello)
thread.start()
thread.join()  # Wait for the thread to finish
print("Hello from main")
```

8.3 Thread Synchronization Techniques

When multiple threads access shared data or resources, there's a risk of **race conditions**, where threads interfere with each other and produce incorrect results. To avoid race conditions, synchronization is necessary.

8.3.1 LOCKS

A **lock** is a synchronization primitive that ensures that only one thread can access a particular section of code at a time. In C, locks can be implemented using `pthread_mutex_t`, in Java with the `synchronized` keyword or `ReentrantLock`, and in Python with the `Lock` object from the `threading` module.

Example in Python:

```python
import threading

lock = threading.Lock()

def critical_section():
    with lock:   # Acquire lock before entering
critical section
        print("Thread is in critical section")

threads = [threading.Thread(target=critical_section)
for _ in range(5)]
for thread in threads:
    thread.start()
for thread in threads:
    thread.join()
```

8.3.2 SEMAPHORES

A **semaphore** is a signaling mechanism that can be used to limit access to a shared resource. It can be used to control the number of threads that can access a resource concurrently.

8.3.3 CONDITION VARIABLES

A **condition variable** allows threads to communicate with each other by waiting for a certain condition to be met. It is often used for producer-consumer problems.

8.4 Concurrent Programming and the Global Interpreter Lock (GIL) in Python

8.4.1 THE GIL IN PYTHON

The **Global Interpreter Lock (GIL)** is a mutex in Python that allows only one thread to execute Python bytecodes at a time. This means that in **CPython** (the most common Python implementation), threads cannot take full advantage of multi-core processors for CPU-bound tasks.

- **Impact on Performance**: For CPU-bound tasks, the GIL limits the effectiveness of threads because only one thread can execute at any given time. For I/O-bound tasks (such as network requests or file I/O), Python threads work well because the GIL is released during blocking I/O operations.
- **Alternatives to Threads**: For CPU-bound tasks, **multiprocessing** (using multiple processes instead of threads) is a better option in Python. Each process runs

independently and has its own memory space, thus bypassing the GIL.

Example using the `multiprocessing` module in Python:

```python
import multiprocessing

def compute():
    print("Computing")

if __name__ == '__main__':
    processes =
[multiprocessing.Process(target=compute) for _ in
range(4)]
    for p in processes:
        p.start()
    for p in processes:
        p.join()
```

8.4.2 WORKAROUNDS FOR THE GIL

For I/O-bound tasks, Python's **threading** module is still useful, as it allows multiple threads to execute while the GIL is released during blocking operations. For CPU-bound tasks, using **multiprocessing** or switching to **Jython** (which doesn't have a GIL) or **IronPython** may be more appropriate.

8.5 Java Concurrency Utilities and the Executor Framework

Java provides a rich set of concurrency utilities, including the **Executor framework**, which simplifies the management of threads.

8.5.1 EXECUTOR FRAMEWORK

The **Executor framework** in Java abstracts the creation, scheduling, and execution of tasks. It provides a higher-level API for concurrent programming compared to directly managing threads.

- **ExecutorService**: Manages a pool of threads and provides methods for submitting tasks and shutting down the executor.
- **ThreadPoolExecutor**: A more advanced implementation that can be used to fine-tune thread management.

Example using **ExecutorService**:

```java
import java.util.concurrent.*;

public class Main {
    public static void main(String[] args) {
        ExecutorService executor =
Executors.newFixedThreadPool(3);

        Runnable task = () ->
System.out.println("Hello from thread: " +
Thread.currentThread().getName());

        for (int i = 0; i < 5; i++) {
            executor.submit(task);   // Submit tasks
to the executor
        }

        executor.shutdown();   // Gracefully shut down
the executor
    }
}
```

In this example:

- The `ExecutorService` manages a fixed-size thread pool of 3 threads.
- Tasks are submitted and executed concurrently.

8.6 Hands-On Example: Write a Multithreaded Program in Java and Python to Perform Concurrent Tasks

8.6.1 JAVA EXAMPLE: MULTITHREADING FOR PARALLEL TASKS

Let's write a Java program that calculates the sum of numbers in parallel using multiple threads.

java

```java
public class SumTask implements Runnable {
    private int start, end;
    private long result = 0;

    public SumTask(int start, int end) {
        this.start = start;
        this.end = end;
    }

    @Override
    public void run() {
        for (int i = start; i <= end; i++) {
            result += i;
        }
    }

    public long getResult() {
        return result;
    }

    public static void main(String[] args) throws
InterruptedException {
```

```java
        int n = 1000;
        int numberOfThreads = 4;
        int range = n / numberOfThreads;

        ExecutorService executor =
Executors.newFixedThreadPool(numberOfThreads);
        SumTask[] tasks = new
SumTask[numberOfThreads];

        for (int i = 0; i < numberOfThreads; i++) {
            int start = i * range + 1;
            int end = (i + 1) * range;
            tasks[i] = new SumTask(start, end);
            executor.submit(tasks[i]);
        }

        executor.shutdown();
        while (!executor.isTerminated()) {}

        long totalSum = 0;
        for (SumTask task : tasks) {
            totalSum += task.getResult();
        }

        System.out.println("Total sum: " + totalSum);
    }
}
```

This Java program divides the sum of numbers from 1 to 1000 into multiple tasks, each handled by a separate thread. After the threads complete their work, the results are combined to get the total sum.

8.6.2 PYTHON EXAMPLE: MULTITHREADING FOR PARALLEL TASKS

Let's write a similar Python program using the `threading` module:

```python
python

import threading

class SumTask(threading.Thread):
```

```python
    def __init__(self, start, end):
        super().__init__()
        self.start = start
        self.end = end
        self.result = 0

    def run(self):
        for i in range(self.start, self.end + 1):
            self.result += i

    def get_result(self):
        return self.result

def main():
    n = 1000
    number_of_threads = 4
    range_size = n // number_of_threads
    threads = []

    for i in range(number_of_threads):
        start = i * range_size + 1
        end = (i + 1) * range_size
        thread = SumTask(start, end)
        threads.append(thread)
        thread.start()

    total_sum = 0
    for thread in threads:
        thread.join()
        total_sum += thread.get_result()

    print("Total sum:", total_sum)

if __name__ == "__main__":
    main()
```

This Python program uses threads to calculate the sum of numbers from 1 to 1000 in parallel. Each thread computes part of the sum, and the main thread collects the results.

8.7 Conclusion

Concurrency and parallelism are powerful techniques for improving the performance and responsiveness of applications. While concurrency allows programs to handle multiple tasks at once, parallelism takes it further by executing multiple tasks simultaneously. Understanding how to manage threads and processes, handle synchronization, and use frameworks like Java's **ExecutorService** or Python's **threading** module is crucial for writing efficient, scalable applications.

By mastering the principles of concurrency and parallelism, you'll be equipped to tackle a wide range of performance-critical problems, from handling concurrent web requests to optimizing computationally intensive tasks.

Chapter 9: Microservices Architecture and High-Level Languages

Objective:

In this chapter, we will introduce the concept of **microservices** and explore how high-level programming languages like **Java**, **Python**, and **Go** are used to implement and support this architecture. Microservices are a modern approach to software architecture, where a large application is broken down into smaller, independent services that can be developed, deployed, and scaled independently. We will discuss the **benefits** and **challenges** of using a microservices architecture, how to design **RESTful APIs**, and how to utilize **Docker** to containerize these services. By the end of this chapter, you will have a solid understanding of microservices and be able to build a simple microservices-based application using **Python** and **Flask**.

9.1 Introduction to Microservices

Microservices is an architectural style that structures a software application as a collection of small, loosely coupled, independently deployable services. Each service in a microservices architecture is responsible for a specific piece of functionality and operates independently of the others.

9.1.1 WHAT ARE MICROSERVICES?

Microservices break down an application into a series of **independent services**. Each service typically has its own database, handles a specific business function, and communicates with other services through **well-defined APIs** (Application Programming Interfaces). Microservices are typically designed around business capabilities and are deployed in a way that allows them to scale independently.

For example, an e-commerce platform could be divided into several microservices like:

- **User Authentication**
- **Product Catalog**
- **Payment Processing**
- **Order Management**
- **Inventory Management**

Each service handles a specific task and is developed, deployed, and scaled independently. This allows for flexibility, agility, and scalability.

9.1.2 BENEFITS OF MICROSERVICES

The primary benefits of a microservices architecture include:

- **Scalability**: Services can be scaled independently based on demand. For instance, you can scale only the **order processing** service during peak times without affecting other services.
- **Flexibility**: Each microservice can be developed in different programming languages or frameworks that best suit the service's specific requirements.

- **Resilience:** If one service fails, it doesn't bring down the entire system. Services can fail gracefully, and the system can continue to operate as other services are still functional.
- **Faster Development:** Smaller services can be developed and deployed more quickly, enabling faster iterations and continuous delivery.

9.1.3 CHALLENGES OF MICROSERVICES

While microservices provide significant benefits, they also come with challenges:

- **Complexity:** Managing multiple services can become complex, especially in large applications. Each service requires its own deployment pipeline, database, and monitoring, increasing operational complexity.
- **Data Management:** Each microservice may have its own database, which can lead to data consistency issues. Ensuring that data is consistent across services can be challenging.
- **Inter-Service Communication:** Microservices need to communicate with each other, often over the network. This introduces latency and can make communication between services complex.
- **Testing and Debugging:** Testing microservices can be difficult, especially when they interact with each other. It requires integration testing, mock services, and complex test setups.

Despite these challenges, microservices have become increasingly popular in large-scale applications due to the advantages they offer in terms of scalability, resilience, and flexibility.

9.2 How High-Level Languages Support Microservices

Different high-level languages like **Java**, **Python**, and **Go** offer various features that make them suitable for developing microservices. Each language has its own strengths when it comes to microservices development, such as scalability, ease of use, and community support.

9.2.1 MICROSERVICES IN JAVA

Java has long been a popular choice for building enterprise applications, and it continues to be widely used for **microservices** because of its **robust frameworks**, **scalability**, and **strong support for concurrency**.

- **Spring Boot**: One of the most popular frameworks for building microservices in Java is **Spring Boot**. Spring Boot allows developers to create stand-alone, production-ready applications with minimal setup. It integrates well with other Spring ecosystem projects like Spring Cloud, which provides tools for distributed systems and service discovery.
- **Java Virtual Machine (JVM)**: Java's portability, thanks to the **JVM**, makes it a good fit for building microservices that need to run across multiple environments.
- **Scalability**: Java's powerful threading and concurrency models make it well-suited for handling high volumes of requests and scaling services independently.

Java-based microservices often interact using **RESTful APIs** and are deployed using containers like **Docker**, enabling independent scaling and management.

9.2.2 Microservices in Python

Python's simplicity and ease of use have made it a popular choice for building microservices, especially in fast-paced development environments where rapid iteration is needed. Python's dynamic nature makes it easy to build APIs, handle data processing, and integrate with other systems.

- **Flask and Django**: Python frameworks like **Flask** and **Django** are commonly used to build microservices. Flask is lightweight and ideal for small, independent services, while Django is a more full-featured framework that can be used for larger applications.
- **Asynchronous Programming**: Python supports asynchronous programming, which makes it easier to handle multiple tasks concurrently without blocking execution. This is particularly useful in microservices where services need to handle multiple requests concurrently.
- **REST APIs**: Python can easily be used to create RESTful APIs using libraries like **Flask-RESTful** or **FastAPI**, allowing microservices to communicate with each other via HTTP.

While Python may not be as fast as Java or Go for CPU-bound tasks, it is an excellent choice for building APIs, handling background tasks, and integrating with other services.

9.2.3 Microservices in Go

Go (or **Golang**) is a modern programming language designed by Google that emphasizes simplicity, concurrency, and performance. Go is particularly suited for building microservices because of its **lightweight concurrency model** and **efficient execution**.

- **Goroutines and Channels**: Go's built-in **goroutines** allow concurrent execution of tasks with minimal overhead. This makes Go an excellent choice for building highly concurrent microservices that can handle multiple tasks simultaneously.

- **Fast Execution**: Go is a compiled language, which means it runs faster than interpreted languages like Python. This makes it suitable for performance-critical microservices.
- **Standard Library**: Go's standard library provides everything needed to build microservices, from handling HTTP requests to working with JSON and performing concurrency. This minimizes the need for external dependencies.

Go is often used for building high-performance, scalable microservices, especially when speed and concurrency are critical factors.

9.3 RESTful APIs and Building Scalable Services

In a microservices architecture, communication between services is often done through **RESTful APIs**. REST (Representational State Transfer) is an architectural style that defines a set of constraints for creating stateless, scalable web services. RESTful APIs use HTTP methods (GET, POST, PUT, DELETE) to allow services to communicate over the network.

9.3.1 WHAT ARE RESTFUL APIS?

A **RESTful API** is an API that adheres to the principles of REST. It is stateless, meaning that each request contains all the information needed for the server to process it. RESTful APIs allow microservices to interact in a simple and standardized way, typically over HTTP.

- **Stateless Communication**: Each request from a client contains all the necessary data to perform the operation, so the server does not need to store any state information between requests.
- **Resource-Based**: In REST, data is treated as resources that can be manipulated using standard HTTP methods.
- **JSON as the Data Format**: RESTful APIs commonly use **JSON** as the data format for communication, making it lightweight and easy to parse.

9.3.2 BUILDING RESTFUL APIS WITH FLASK IN PYTHON

Python's **Flask** framework is often used to build microservices that expose RESTful APIs. Flask provides a simple way to define routes, handle requests, and return responses.

Example of a simple RESTful API using **Flask**:

```python
from flask import Flask, jsonify

app = Flask(__name__)

# Sample data
tasks = [
    {"id": 1, "title": "Buy groceries", "done":
False},
    {"id": 2, "title": "Walk the dog", "done": True}
]

@app.route('/tasks', methods=['GET'])
def get_tasks():
    return jsonify(tasks)

if __name__ == '__main__':
    app.run(debug=True)
```

This Flask application defines a route `/tasks` that returns a list of tasks in **JSON** format. This simple microservice exposes a RESTful API that could be consumed by other services in the system.

9.4 Using Docker for Microservices Development

Docker is a platform used to create, deploy, and manage containers. A **container** is a lightweight, standalone, executable package of software that includes everything needed to run a service, such as the code, runtime, libraries, and system dependencies.

In the context of microservices, Docker allows each service to run in its own isolated container, making it easier to develop, deploy, and scale services independently.

9.4.1 WHY USE DOCKER WITH MICROSERVICES?

- **Isolation**: Each microservice runs in its own container, which ensures that services do not interfere with each other and that dependencies are kept isolated.
- **Portability**: Docker containers can be run on any machine that has Docker installed, making it easy to move services between development, staging, and production environments.
- **Scalability**: Containers can be easily scaled up or down based on demand, making it easy to manage traffic loads and performance requirements.

9.4.2 DOCKERIZING A PYTHON FLASK MICROSERVICE

Here's how you can containerize the Flask microservice we created earlier:

1. **Create a Dockerfile:** A `Dockerfile` defines the steps to build a Docker image for your service.

```
Dockerfile

# Use the official Python image as the base
FROM python:3.9-slim

# Set the working directory
WORKDIR /app

#  the requirements.txt file and install dependencies
 requirements.txt .
RUN pip install -r requirements.txt

#  the application code into the container
 . .

# Expose the application port
EXPOSE 5000

# Run the Flask app
CMD ["python", "app.py"]
```

2. **Build and Run the Docker Container:**

```bash
bash

# Build the Docker image
docker build -t flask-microservice .

# Run the container
docker run -p 5000:5000 flask-microservice
```

Your Flask microservice is now running inside a Docker container, making it portable and easily deployable.

9.5 Hands-On Example: Develop a Simple Microservices-Based Application Using Python and Flask

Let's now build a simple **microservices-based application** using **Python**, **Flask**, and **Docker**. We will create two microservices: one for managing tasks and another for user authentication. These two services will communicate via RESTful APIs.

STEP 1: TASK SERVICE (FLASK API)

This service will manage a list of tasks and expose an API to fetch and update them.

```python
from flask import Flask, jsonify, request

app = Flask(__name__)

tasks = [
    {"id": 1, "title": "Buy groceries", "done": False},
    {"id": 2, "title": "Walk the dog", "done": True}
]

@app.route('/tasks', methods=['GET'])
def get_tasks():
    return jsonify(tasks)

@app.route('/tasks', methods=['POST'])
def add_task():
    task = request.get_json()
    tasks.append(task)
    return jsonify(task), 201
```

```python
if __name__ == '__main__':
    app.run(debug=True, host='0.0.0.0')
```

STEP 2: AUTHENTICATION SERVICE (FLASK API)

This service will simulate user authentication.

```python
python

from flask import Flask, jsonify, request

app = Flask(__name__)

users = [
    {"username": "admin", "password": "password123"}
]

@app.route('/login', methods=['POST'])
def login():
    credentials = request.get_json()
    for user in users:
        if user["username"] ==
credentials["username"] and user["password"] ==
credentials["password"]:
            return jsonify({"message": "Login
successful"}), 200
    return jsonify({"message": "Invalid
credentials"}), 401

if __name__ == '__main__':
    app.run(debug=True, host='0.0.0.0')
```

STEP 3: DOCKERIZING BOTH SERVICES

You can now containerize both services using Docker, following the steps outlined earlier. This allows you to run each service in its own container and deploy them independently.

9.6 Conclusion

Microservices architecture enables developers to create scalable, flexible, and resilient applications by breaking down large systems into smaller, independently deployable services. High-level languages like **Java**, **Python**, and **Go** offer powerful tools and frameworks to build microservices that can communicate with each other through **RESTful APIs**. Additionally, **Docker** provides an efficient way to deploy and manage these services, making them portable and easy to scale.

By leveraging microservices, you can build applications that are more modular, easier to maintain, and more responsive to changing demands. However, it's important to consider the complexity that comes with managing multiple services, handling inter-service communication, and ensuring data consistency.

Chapter 10: Functional Programming and Modern High-Level Languages

Objective:

In this chapter, we will dive into **functional programming** (FP), a programming paradigm that emphasizes the use of functions and immutability to build software in a declarative style. We will explore the rise of functional programming in modern high-level languages such as **Python, Java**, and **JavaScript**, and understand how these languages support and implement FP principles. This chapter will cover **key functional programming concepts** such as **first-class functions, higher-order functions, lambda expressions, map/filter/reduce**, and more. By the end of this chapter, you will be able to recognize functional programming patterns and apply them effectively in different programming languages.

10.1 What is Functional Programming? Key Concepts

Functional programming is a programming paradigm that treats computation as the evaluation of mathematical functions and avoids changing state and mutable data. It is based on **mathematical functions** where the output is determined solely by the input, with no side effects.

There are several key principles that define functional programming:

1. **First-Class and Higher-Order Functions:**
   - In FP, functions are **first-class citizens**, meaning they can be assigned to variables, passed as arguments to other functions, and returned from functions.
   - **Higher-order functions** are functions that either take other functions as arguments or return functions as results.
2. **Immutability:**
   - **Immutability** refers to the idea that once a value is assigned to a variable, it cannot be changed. Instead of modifying variables, functional programs produce new values, which helps reduce side effects and makes the code easier to reason about.
3. **Pure Functions:**
   - A **pure function** is a function where the output is solely determined by the input, without side effects. This means a pure function will always return the same result if given the same input and will not alter any external state.
4. **Declarative Programming:**
   - Functional programming is **declarative**, meaning that it focuses on describing **what** to do rather than **how** to do it. This contrasts with **imperative programming**, where the focus is on describing the exact steps to achieve a goal.
5. **Referential Transparency:**
   - An expression is **referentially transparent** if it can be replaced with its value without changing the program's behavior. This concept ties into pure functions, as they are always referentially transparent.

Functional programming offers several benefits:

- **Modularity and Reusability**: Functions in FP are often smaller and more reusable, leading to cleaner and more maintainable code.
- **Concurrency and Parallelism**: Since functional programs avoid mutable state, they are naturally suited for concurrent and parallel execution.
- **Easier Testing and Debugging**: Pure functions and immutability make it easier to test individual components and track down bugs.
- **Code Simplicity and Predictability**: By avoiding side effects, functional programs are often more predictable and easier to reason about.

While functional programming is powerful, it does require a different mindset than traditional imperative programming. Let's look at how functional programming is implemented in modern high-level languages like Python, Java, and JavaScript.

10.2 Functional Programming in Python

Python is traditionally known as an **imperative** and **object-oriented** language, but over time, it has incorporated functional programming features, making it easier to write **functional-style** code.

10.2.1 LAMBDA FUNCTIONS

One of the core features of functional programming is the ability to use **anonymous functions**, also known as **lambda functions**. A lambda function is a small, one-line function that can be defined without a name.

Example:

```python
python
```

```python
# A simple lambda function to add two numbers
add = lambda x, y: x + y
print(add(3, 4))   # Outputs: 7
```

Lambda functions in Python are useful for short, simple operations where defining a full function might seem overkill.

10.2.2 MAP, FILTER, AND REDUCE

Python provides several built-in functions that support functional programming patterns: **map**, **filter**, and **reduce**.

- `map()` : Applies a function to every item in an iterable and returns a new iterable with the results.
- `filter()` : Filters elements of an iterable based on a function that returns a boolean value.
- `reduce()` (from the `functools` module): Applies a rolling computation to sequential items in an iterable, so as to reduce the iterable to a single value.

Example of using `map()` and `filter()`:

```python
python
```

```python
# Map: Multiply each number in the list by 2
numbers = [1, 2, 3, 4]
doubled = list(map(lambda x: x * 2, numbers))
print(doubled)   # Outputs: [2, 4, 6, 8]

# Filter: Keep only even numbers
```

```python
even_numbers = list(filter(lambda x: x % 2 == 0,
numbers))
print(even_numbers)   # Outputs: [2, 4]
```

10.2.3 USING LIST COMPREHENSIONS

While not strictly functional programming, **list comprehensions** provide a concise, functional-style way to create lists by applying a function to each element of an iterable.

python

```python
# List comprehension to square each number in a list
squares = [x ** 2 for x in numbers]
print(squares)   # Outputs: [1, 4, 9, 16]
```

10.3 Java's Functional Interfaces and Streams

In Java, **functional programming** was introduced with **Java 8**, which brought several features like **lambda expressions, streams**, and **functional interfaces.**

10.3.1 FUNCTIONAL INTERFACES

A **functional interface** is an interface with just one abstract method. These interfaces can be used with lambda expressions to represent single-method interfaces in a more concise and readable manner.

Example of a functional interface:

java

```java
@FunctionalInterface
interface MathOperation {
    int operate(int a, int b);
```

```
}

public class Main {
    public static void main(String[] args) {
        MathOperation add = (a, b) -> a + b;   //
Lambda expression
        System.out.println(add.operate(5, 3));   //
Outputs: 8
    }
}
```

10.3.2 STREAMS API

The **Streams API** is a powerful feature introduced in Java 8 that allows developers to process sequences of data in a functional style. Streams provide methods to filter, map, reduce, and collect data.

Example of using Streams:

```
java

import java.util.*;
import java.util.stream.*;

public class Main {
    public static void main(String[] args) {
        List<Integer> numbers = Arrays.asList(1, 2,
3, 4, 5);

        // Filter even numbers and square them
        List<Integer> result = numbers.stream()
                                       .filter(n -> n
% 2 == 0)
                                       .map(n -> n *
n)
.collect(Collectors.toList());

        System.out.println(result);   // Outputs: [4,
16]
```

```
        }
}
```

In this example, the stream filters even numbers and maps them to their square values, showcasing a functional style of processing collections.

10.4 Comparing Functional and Object-Oriented Programming

Functional programming and object-oriented programming are two of the most prominent paradigms used in modern software development. Each has its strengths and weaknesses, and understanding the differences between them can help you choose the best approach for your project.

10.4.1 KEY DIFFERENCES

- **State and Immutability**: In **functional programming**, the focus is on **immutable data** and **pure functions**, while **object-oriented programming** encourages encapsulation, where the state is stored within objects.
- **Code Structure**: **OOP** is centered around organizing code into objects, which contain both data and methods. **Functional programming**, on the other hand, focuses on **functions** and avoids mutating state.
- **Concurrency: Functional programming** often leads to simpler concurrent programming because there is no mutable state, making it easier to reason about parallel execution. **OOP** may require complex synchronization to handle shared state across objects.

10.4.2 ADVANTAGES OF FUNCTIONAL PROGRAMMING

- **Code Simplicity and Modularity**: Functional programming leads to smaller, reusable functions that can be easily composed and tested.
- **Concurrency**: FP is naturally suited for concurrent programming because of its focus on **immutable data** and **pure functions**.
- **Less Side Effects**: Pure functions have no side effects, making them easier to understand and debug.

10.4.3 ADVANTAGES OF OBJECT-ORIENTED PROGRAMMING

- **Modeling Real-World Entities**: OOP allows you to model real-world entities using objects, making it easier to represent complex systems.
- **Code Reusability**: Through **inheritance**, OOP allows you to reuse code and build upon existing functionality.
- **State Management**: OOP is great for managing the state of complex systems where different entities need to interact and share data.

10.5 Hands-On Example: Convert an Imperative Algorithm to a Functional One in Python

Let's take a simple imperative algorithm and convert it into a functional one using Python. We'll start with an algorithm that finds the sum of squares of even numbers from a list.

Imperative Version (For Loop)

python

```python
numbers = [1, 2, 3, 4, 5, 6, 7, 8, 9]
sum_of_squares = 0

for num in numbers:
    if num % 2 == 0:
        sum_of_squares += num * num

print(sum_of_squares)  # Outputs: 120
```

This is an imperative approach, where we use a `for` loop to iterate through the list and apply conditions.

Functional Version (Using map and filter)

python

```python
numbers = [1, 2, 3, 4, 5, 6, 7, 8, 9]

# Filter even numbers and square them, then sum the
result
sum_of_squares = sum(map(lambda x: x * x,
filter(lambda x: x % 2 == 0, numbers)))

print(sum_of_squares)  # Outputs: 120
```

In the functional version:

- We use `filter()` to extract the even numbers.
- We use `map()` to square the even numbers.
- Finally, we use `sum()` to calculate the sum of the squared numbers.

10.6 Conclusion

Functional programming provides a powerful paradigm for writing clean, modular, and testable code. It emphasizes the use of **pure functions, immutability**, and **higher-order functions**, which can lead to more predictable and maintainable applications. High-level languages like **Python, Java**, and **JavaScript** have adopted functional programming features, making it easier to integrate functional patterns into modern software development.

While **object-oriented programming** remains dominant in many large systems due to its ability to model real-world entities and manage state, **functional programming** is gaining popularity for its simplicity, concurrency-friendly nature, and ease of testing. By understanding both paradigms, developers can choose the best approach for their specific use case.

Chapter 11: High-Level Programming in Web Development

Objective:

This chapter explores the role of **high-level programming languages** in **web development**, covering both **server-side** and **client-side** programming. We will discuss the fundamentals of **full-stack development**, focusing on languages like **Java, Python**, and **Node.js**. We will also dive into popular **JavaScript frameworks** such as **React** and **Vue**, which are used for building dynamic and responsive user interfaces. The chapter will explore **frontend** and **backend integration** and conclude with a hands-on example of creating a simple web application using **Python Flask** for the backend and **HTML/JavaScript** for the frontend.

11.1 Introduction to Web Development

Web development has evolved dramatically over the past few decades, transitioning from basic static pages to complex, dynamic, and interactive web applications. Modern web development is often divided into two major components: the **frontend** (client-side) and the **backend** (server-side). Understanding how these components work together is essential for building efficient, scalable, and maintainable web applications.

11.1.1 What is Full-Stack Development?

Full-stack development refers to the practice of developing both the frontend and the backend of a web application. A **full-stack developer** is someone who is proficient in both **client-side** and **server-side** technologies, allowing them to build end-to-end solutions.

In **high-level programming** for web development, full-stack developers typically work with languages and frameworks that simplify both the client-side and server-side development. The following sections will break down how high-level languages like **Java**, **Python**, and **JavaScript** are used in both the frontend and backend of modern web applications.

11.2 Server-Side vs. Client-Side Programming

Understanding the distinction between **server-side** and **client-side programming** is fundamental to modern web development.

11.2.1 Server-Side Programming

Server-side programming refers to operations that are performed on the web server. The server processes requests from clients (users) and generates the appropriate responses, which can include serving static content, querying databases, or performing complex computations.

- **Key Characteristics of Server-Side Programming**:
    - **Data Processing**: The server handles tasks like querying databases, processing data, and executing business logic.

- o **Dynamic Content**: Server-side languages generate dynamic web pages based on the data and logic, such as personalized dashboards or user accounts.
- o **Languages**: Common server-side languages include **Java**, **Python**, **PHP**, **Ruby**, and **Node.js**.
- o **Databases**: Server-side applications often interact with databases (e.g., **MySQL**, **PostgreSQL**, or **MongoDB**) to store and retrieve data.

11.2.2 CLIENT-SIDE PROGRAMMING

Client-side programming, on the other hand, involves operations that are performed on the user's web browser. The client is responsible for rendering content, handling user interactions, and communicating with the server.

- • **Key Characteristics of Client-Side Programming**:
  - o **User Interface**: The client is responsible for displaying the content and providing an interactive user interface (UI).
  - o **Real-Time Updates**: JavaScript is used to update the UI without requiring a full page reload, providing a smooth user experience.
  - o **Languages**: The primary language for client-side programming is **JavaScript**, though **HTML** and **CSS** are also crucial for structuring and styling web pages.

11.2.3 THE RELATIONSHIP BETWEEN SERVER-SIDE AND CLIENT-SIDE

While server-side programming handles the data and business logic, client-side programming focuses on presenting that data to users and handling interactions. The two communicate via **HTTP requests** and **APIs,** with client-side applications making requests to the server for data, and the server returning data to be rendered on the frontend.

11.3 Full-Stack Development with Java, Python, and Node.js

High-level languages like **Java**, **Python**, and **Node.js** each have strengths when it comes to full-stack web development. These languages offer frameworks and tools that simplify building both server-side and client-side components of web applications.

11.3.1 JAVA FOR FULL-STACK DEVELOPMENT

Java has long been a dominant language for enterprise-level applications, and its extensive ecosystem makes it a solid choice for both server-side and client-side development.

- **Backend with Java: Spring Boot** is the most commonly used framework for building server-side applications in Java. It simplifies the development of RESTful APIs, database interactions, and security.
- **Frontend with Java**: While Java is primarily a backend language, frameworks like **JavaFX** can be used for building rich desktop-like applications. However, in web development, Java is rarely used directly for frontend work. Instead, developers use **JavaScript** for the frontend, but Java applets (deprecated) were historically used for some interactive web elements.

Example: In Java, a typical full-stack application might involve **Spring Boot** for the backend (serving APIs, handling user authentication, interacting with databases) and **JavaScript frameworks** (like **React**) for the frontend.

11.3.2 PYTHON FOR FULL-STACK DEVELOPMENT

Python is a popular language for web development due to its simplicity and readability. It is often used in the backend to handle business logic, process data, and interact with databases.

- **Backend with Python**: **Flask** and **Django** are two of the most popular Python frameworks for building web applications. Flask is lightweight and ideal for small to medium-sized applications, while Django is more feature-rich and suited for larger, more complex systems.
- **Frontend with Python**: Python is rarely used for client-side development in web applications. However, frameworks like **Brython** aim to run Python directly in the browser, but the standard for frontend work remains **JavaScript**.

Example: In Python, a full-stack application might use **Flask** for the backend and **HTML/JavaScript** for the frontend, with the data being communicated via **RESTful APIs**.

11.3.3 NODE.JS FOR FULL-STACK DEVELOPMENT

Node.js is a runtime environment for running JavaScript on the server side. It has become increasingly popular for building both backend and frontend components of full-stack web applications.

- **Backend with Node.js**: **Express.js** is the most commonly used Node.js framework for building RESTful APIs, handling HTTP requests, and interacting with databases.
- **Frontend with Node.js**: Node.js uses **JavaScript** for both backend and frontend development. With tools like **React**, **Vue**, and **Angular**, developers can build dynamic, single-page applications (SPAs) that provide a rich user experience.

Example: A full-stack application built with **Node.js** might use **Express.js** for the backend, **MongoDB** for the database, and **React** for the frontend, all written in JavaScript.

11.4 Using JavaScript Frameworks Like React and Vue

11.4.1 REACT

React is one of the most popular JavaScript frameworks for building dynamic user interfaces. It allows developers to create reusable UI components that can efficiently update and render data. React uses a **virtual DOM** to improve performance by minimizing direct manipulation of the real DOM.

- **Key Features of React:**
    - **Components**: React applications are built using components, which are self-contained pieces of UI that can be reused throughout the application.
    - **State Management**: React allows you to manage state within components, providing an interactive experience for users.
    - **Hooks**: React introduced hooks in version 16.8, allowing developers to manage state and side effects in functional components.

Example: A simple React component:

```javascript
import React, { useState } from 'react';

function Counter() {
```

```
    const [count, setCount] = useState(0);

    return (
        <div>
            <p>You clicked {count} times</p>
            <button onClick={() => setCount(count +
1)}>Click me</button>
        </div>
    );
}

export default Counter;
```

In this example, `useState` manages the state of the counter, and the `button` click handler updates the state, causing the component to re-render.

11.4.2 VUE

Vue.js is another popular JavaScript framework that focuses on building user interfaces and single-page applications. It is known for its simplicity and flexibility, making it easy to integrate with other projects.

- **Key Features of Vue:**
    - o **Declarative Rendering**: Vue uses a template syntax that allows developers to declaratively bind data to the DOM.
    - o **Reactivity**: Vue's reactivity system ensures that changes in data automatically update the UI.
    - o **Single-File Components**: Vue allows developers to write templates, scripts, and styles in a single .vue file.

Example: A simple Vue component:

```
html
```

```
<template>
  <div>
    <p>You clicked {{ count }} times</p>
    <button @click="increment">Click me</button>
  </div>
</template>

<script>
export default {
  data() {
    return {
      count: 0
    };
  },
  methods: {
    increment() {
      this.count++;
    }
  }
};
</script>

<style scoped>
button {
  padding: 10px;
  font-size: 16px;
}
</style>
```

In this example, Vue's **data binding** automatically updates the UI when the count value changes.

11.5 Frontend and Backend Integration

Frontend and backend integration is key to building dynamic, full-stack web applications. The frontend interacts with the backend through **APIs** (Application Programming Interfaces), typically in the form of **RESTful APIs** or **GraphQL APIs**.

11.5.1 RESTFUL APIS FOR INTEGRATION

A **RESTful API** is an architectural style for designing networked applications. It relies on stateless communication and uses standard HTTP methods like **GET, POST, PUT,** and **DELETE** to perform operations on resources.

- **Frontend to Backend Communication**: The frontend sends HTTP requests (typically using **AJAX** or **fetch()**) to interact with the backend. The backend processes the request, interacts with the database, and returns the appropriate response.

Example of Frontend to Backend API Communication:

```javascript
// Frontend (React or Vue)
fetch('https://api.example.com/tasks', {
  method: 'GET',
})
  .then(response => response.json())
  .then(data => console.log(data));

// Backend (Flask)
from flask import Flask, jsonify

app = Flask(__name__)

@app.route('/tasks', methods=['GET'])
def get_tasks():
    tasks = [{"id": 1, "task": "Buy groceries"}]
    return jsonify(tasks)

if __name__ == '__main__':
    app.run(debug=True)
```

In this example, the frontend sends a **GET** request to the backend to fetch tasks, and the backend responds with a JSON list of tasks.

11.6 Hands-On Example: Create a Simple Web App Using Python Flask for the Backend and HTML/JavaScript for the Frontend

Let's build a simple web application with **Python Flask** for the backend and **HTML/JavaScript** for the frontend. The app will allow users to add tasks and display them in a list.

STEP 1: SET UP THE BACKEND (FLASK)

First, create a simple backend with Flask to serve tasks and allow adding new ones:

```python
python

from flask import Flask, jsonify, request

app = Flask(__name__)

tasks = [{"id": 1, "task": "Learn Flask"}]

@app.route('/tasks', methods=['GET'])
def get_tasks():
    return jsonify(tasks)

@app.route('/tasks', methods=['POST'])
def add_task():
    new_task = request.get_json()
    tasks.append(new_task)
    return jsonify(new_task), 201

if __name__ == '__main__':
    app.run(debug=True)
```

Next, create the frontend using HTML and JavaScript to interact with the Flask API:

html

```html
<!DOCTYPE html>
<html lang="en">
<head>
  <meta charset="UTF-8">
  <meta name="viewport" content="width=device-width,
initial-scale=1.0">
  <title>Task Manager</title>
</head>
<body>
  <h1>Task Manager</h1>
  <ul id="task-list"></ul>
  <input type="text" id="task-input"
placeholder="Enter new task">
  <button onclick="addTask()">Add Task</button>

  <script>
    // Fetch tasks from the backend
    function fetchTasks() {
      fetch('/tasks')
        .then(response => response.json())
        .then(data => {
          const taskList =
document.getElementById('task-list');
          taskList.innerHTML = '';
          data.forEach(task => {
            const li = document.createElement('li');
            li.textContent = task.task;
            taskList.appendChild(li);
          });
        });
    }

    // Add a new task
    function addTask() {
      const taskInput =
document.getElementById('task-input');
```

```
      const newTask = { task: taskInput.value };

      fetch('/tasks', {
        method: 'POST',
        headers: {
          'Content-Type': 'application/json',
        },
        body: JSON.stringify(newTask),
      })
        .then(response => response.json())
        .then(() => {
          taskInput.value = '';
          fetchTasks();
        });
    }

    // Initial fetch
    fetchTasks();
  </script>
</body>
</html>
```

In this simple app:

- The **Flask backend** serves a list of tasks and allows adding new ones.
- The **frontend** (HTML and JavaScript) interacts with the backend using **fetch()** to get tasks and send new ones.

11.7 Conclusion

High-level programming languages like **Java, Python**, and **JavaScript** play a pivotal role in modern web development. **Full-stack development** with these languages allows developers to build both the frontend and backend of web applications efficiently. While **JavaScript frameworks** like **React** and **Vue** provide powerful tools for building dynamic user interfaces, **Python** and **Java** offer robust frameworks for building scalable server-side applications. By using **RESTful APIs** and tools like **Docker** to containerize services, developers can build scalable and maintainable web applications that meet the demands of today's fast-paced web environments.

Chapter 12: High-Level Languages in Data Science and Machine Learning

Objective:

This chapter explores the use of **high-level programming languages** in the fields of **data science** and **machine learning**. We will discuss how languages like **Python** and **Java** play an essential role in data manipulation, statistical analysis, and the development of predictive models. We will cover popular **Python libraries** for data science, such as **Pandas, NumPy**, and **Matplotlib**, and explore machine learning frameworks like **TensorFlow** and **Scikit-learn**. Additionally, we will discuss how **Java** is used for big data processing and give an example of how to build a simple **machine learning model** in Python to predict housing prices. By the end of this chapter, you will have a solid understanding of how high-level programming languages are integral to data science and machine learning workflows.

12.1 Introduction to Data Science and Machine Learning

Data science and machine learning have become essential fields of study as industries and organizations increasingly rely on data to drive decisions and gain insights. These fields combine knowledge from statistics, computer science, and domain expertise to analyze and model data in a way that can help solve complex problems.

- **Data Science** is the process of extracting meaningful insights from structured and unstructured data. It involves data collection, cleaning, exploration, analysis, and visualization.
- **Machine Learning (ML)** is a subset of artificial intelligence (AI) that focuses on developing algorithms that allow computers to learn from and make predictions based on data, without being explicitly programmed for every task.

High-level programming languages are central to both data science and machine learning. Their rich ecosystems of libraries and frameworks provide the tools necessary to handle complex tasks such as **data manipulation**, **visualization**, **model training**, and **model deployment**.

12.2 Python Libraries for Data Science

Python is widely considered the best language for data science, and for good reason. Its simplicity, readability, and the availability of a wide range of libraries make it an ideal choice for both beginners and experts.

12.2.1 PANDAS

Pandas is a powerful library in Python used for data manipulation and analysis. It provides two main data structures: **Series** (1-dimensional) and **DataFrame** (2-dimensional), which are used to hold and manipulate data.

- **Key Features of Pandas**:
  - **DataFrames**: The DataFrame is a 2D structure that can hold heterogeneous data types (e.g., integers,

strings, floats). It is similar to a table in a relational database or an Excel spreadsheet.
- o **Data Cleaning**: Pandas provides robust tools for handling missing data, duplicates, and various data transformation tasks.
- o **Data Aggregation and Grouping**: You can group data and apply aggregate functions like `sum()`, `mean()`, or `count()` to each group.
- o **Merging and Joining**: Pandas supports SQL-like operations for merging or joining multiple datasets together.

Example of using Pandas:

python

```python
import pandas as pd

# Create a DataFrame
data = {'Name': ['John', 'Anna', 'Peter', 'Linda'],
'Age': [28, 24, 35, 32]}
df = pd.DataFrame(data)

# DataFrame manipulation
df['Age'] = df['Age'] + 1  # Increase age by 1 year
print(df)
```

12.2.2 NUMPY

NumPy is another essential Python library, particularly for numerical computations. It provides support for arrays, matrices, and multi-dimensional data structures, as well as mathematical functions to operate on these arrays.

- **Key Features of NumPy**:
  - o **N-dimensional Arrays**: NumPy arrays are more efficient than Python's native lists when performing mathematical operations.

- o **Mathematical Functions**: NumPy offers a wide range of functions to perform vectorized operations on arrays, such as element-wise addition, multiplication, and advanced linear algebra operations.
- o **Random Sampling**: NumPy's random module supports generating random numbers and sampling from distributions, which is crucial for simulating data in machine learning.

Example of using NumPy:

```python
python

import numpy as np

# Create a NumPy array
arr = np.array([1, 2, 3, 4, 5])

# Perform mathematical operations
arr_squared = np.square(arr)
print(arr_squared)
```

12.2.3 MATPLOTLIB

Matplotlib is a powerful library for **data visualization**. It allows you to create static, animated, and interactive plots and charts, including line plots, bar charts, histograms, and scatter plots.

- **Key Features of Matplotlib:**
  - o **Customizable Plots**: You can customize almost every aspect of your plots, including titles, axes labels, legends, and colors.
  - o **Subplots**: Matplotlib supports the creation of subplots, enabling you to display multiple visualizations on the same figure.

- o **Integration with Pandas**: Matplotlib integrates well with Pandas DataFrames, allowing you to directly plot data from DataFrames.

Example of using Matplotlib:

```python
import matplotlib.pyplot as plt

# Create some data
x = [1, 2, 3, 4, 5]
y = [2, 3, 5, 7, 11]

# Plot the data
plt.plot(x, y)
plt.title('Prime Numbers Plot')
plt.xlabel('X-axis')
plt.ylabel('Y-axis')
plt.show()
```

12.3 Using Machine Learning Frameworks: TensorFlow, Scikit-learn

Python offers several powerful machine learning frameworks that simplify the process of developing machine learning models. Two of the most commonly used frameworks are **TensorFlow** and **Scikit-learn**.

12.3.1 SCIKIT-LEARN

Scikit-learn is a simple and efficient library for data mining and machine learning. It provides easy-to-use tools for building and evaluating models, and it is particularly well-suited for classical machine learning tasks such as classification, regression, clustering, and dimensionality reduction.

- **Key Features of Scikit-learn:**
  - **Preprocessing**: Scikit-learn includes utilities for data scaling, encoding categorical variables, and splitting datasets into training and testing sets.
  - **Modeling**: The library includes implementations of a wide range of algorithms, such as **decision trees, support vector machines, logistic regression**, and **k-nearest neighbors**.
  - **Model Evaluation**: Scikit-learn provides tools for evaluating models using techniques such as **cross-validation** and **grid search** for hyperparameter tuning.

Example of using Scikit-learn:

python

```
from sklearn.datasets import load_boston
from sklearn.model_selection import train_test_split
from sklearn.linear_model import LinearRegression
from sklearn.metrics import mean_squared_error

# Load dataset
data = load_boston()
X = data.data
y = data.target

# Split data into training and test sets
X_train, X_test, y_train, y_test =
train_test_split(X, y, test_size=0.2,
random_state=42)

# Train a model
model = LinearRegression()
model.fit(X_train, y_train)

# Make predictions and evaluate the model
y_pred = model.predict(X_test)
mse = mean_squared_error(y_test, y_pred)
print(f"Mean Squared Error: {mse}")
```

12.3.2 TENSORFLOW

TensorFlow is an open-source library for **machine learning** and **deep learning** developed by Google. It is primarily used for building and training complex neural networks and is one of the most popular frameworks in the AI community.

- **Key Features of TensorFlow**:
  - **Keras**: TensorFlow includes Keras, a high-level neural networks API, which simplifies the creation of deep learning models.
  - **TensorFlow Lite**: TensorFlow provides tools for deploying models on mobile and embedded devices through **TensorFlow Lite**.
  - **GPU Support**: TensorFlow can utilize **GPUs** for faster model training, especially for large datasets and deep learning tasks.

Example of using TensorFlow:

python

```python
import tensorflow as tf
from tensorflow.keras.models import Sequential
from tensorflow.keras.layers import Dense
from tensorflow.keras.datasets import mnist

# Load MNIST dataset
(x_train, y_train), (x_test, y_test) =
mnist.load_data()

# Preprocess the data
x_train = x_train.reshape((x_train.shape[0], 28, 28,
1)) / 255.0
x_test = x_test.reshape((x_test.shape[0], 28, 28, 1))
/ 255.0

# Create a simple CNN model
model = Sequential([
```

```
    tf.keras.layers.Conv2D(32, (3, 3),
activation='relu', input_shape=(28, 28, 1)),
    tf.keras.layers.MaxPooling2D((2, 2)),
    tf.keras.layers.Flatten(),
    tf.keras.layers.Dense(128, activation='relu'),
    tf.keras.layers.Dense(10, activation='softmax')
])

# Compile and train the model
model.compile(optimizer='adam',
loss='sparse_categorical_crossentropy',
metrics=['accuracy'])
model.fit(x_train, y_train, epochs=5)

# Evaluate the model
model.evaluate(x_test, y_test)
```

12.4 Data Visualization and Analysis in Python

Data visualization is a key component of data analysis. By using Python's powerful libraries, we can not only analyze data but also create insightful and visually appealing charts and plots that help in understanding the patterns and trends.

12.4.1 VISUALIZING DATA WITH MATPLOTLIB

As discussed earlier, **Matplotlib** is a powerful library for creating static, animated, and interactive plots in Python. It allows you to create a wide range of visualizations such as line plots, bar charts, histograms, scatter plots, and more.

12.4.2 SEABORN FOR STATISTICAL PLOTS

Seaborn is built on top of Matplotlib and provides a high-level interface for drawing attractive and informative statistical graphics.

It simplifies the process of creating complex plots like heatmaps, pair plots, and violin plots.

Example of using Seaborn:

```python
python

import seaborn as sns
import matplotlib.pyplot as plt

# Load the Iris dataset
iris = sns.load_dataset("iris")

# Create a pair plot
sns.pairplot(iris, hue="species")
plt.show()
```

12.4.3 PLOTLY FOR INTERACTIVE VISUALIZATIONS

Plotly is a popular library for creating interactive visualizations. It is especially useful for building dashboards or applications that require user interaction, such as zooming and clicking.

Example of using Plotly:

```python
python

import plotly.express as px

# Create an interactive scatter plot
fig = px.scatter(iris, x="sepal_length",
y="sepal_width", color="species")
fig.show()
```

12.5 Big Data Processing in Java

While Python is the dominant language for data science, **Java** also plays an important role in processing **big data**. Java is particularly useful when dealing with large-scale data that needs to be processed across multiple machines or clusters. Frameworks like **Apache Hadoop** and **Apache Spark** are often used to process big data in distributed environments.

12.5.1 APACHE HADOOP

Apache Hadoop is a framework for distributed storage and processing of large datasets using the **MapReduce** programming model. It is designed to handle massive amounts of data by distributing the workload across multiple nodes in a cluster.

- **MapReduce**: The **MapReduce** model splits a task into two parts: **Map** (which processes data) and **Reduce** (which aggregates the results).

12.5.2 APACHE SPARK

Apache Spark is a fast, in-memory data processing engine that provides a unified framework for big data analytics. Spark is faster than Hadoop for many tasks because it performs in-memory processing, reducing the need for reading/writing to disk.

Spark's **Java API** is widely used for big data processing, and it also supports other languages like **Python, R**, and **Scala**.

12.6 Hands-On Example: Build a Simple Machine Learning Model in Python to Predict Housing Prices

Now, let's put everything into practice and build a **machine learning model** in Python to predict housing prices using the **Scikit-learn** library.

STEP 1: IMPORT NECESSARY LIBRARIES

python

```
import pandas as pd
import numpy as np
from sklearn.model_selection import train_test_split
from sklearn.linear_model import LinearRegression
from sklearn.metrics import mean_squared_error
import matplotlib.pyplot as plt
```

STEP 2: LOAD THE DATASET

For this example, we'll use the **Boston Housing Dataset**, which is a popular dataset for regression tasks.

python

```
from sklearn.datasets import load_boston
boston = load_boston()

# Convert to a pandas DataFrame
df = pd.DataFrame(boston.data,
columns=boston.feature_names)
df['PRICE'] = boston.target
```

STEP 3: PREPARE THE DATA

Split the data into **training** and **test** sets.

```python
X = df.drop('PRICE', axis=1)
y = df['PRICE']

X_train, X_test, y_train, y_test =
train_test_split(X, y, test_size=0.2,
random_state=42)
```

STEP 4: TRAIN THE MODEL

We'll use **Linear Regression** to predict housing prices based on the features.

```python
model = LinearRegression()
model.fit(X_train, y_train)
```

STEP 5: EVALUATE THE MODEL

Make predictions and evaluate the model using **Mean Squared Error (MSE)**.

```python
y_pred = model.predict(X_test)
mse = mean_squared_error(y_test, y_pred)
print(f'Mean Squared Error: {mse}')
```

STEP 6: VISUALIZE THE RESULTS

```python
plt.scatter(y_test, y_pred)
plt.xlabel('True Prices')
plt.ylabel('Predicted Prices')
plt.title('True vs Predicted Prices')
plt.show()
```

12.7 Conclusion

High-level programming languages like **Python** and **Java** play a crucial role in the fields of **data science** and **machine learning**. Python, with its rich ecosystem of libraries like **Pandas**, **NumPy**, **Scikit-learn**, and **TensorFlow**, provides powerful tools for data manipulation, statistical analysis, and model building. On the other hand, **Java** is widely used for big data processing, especially with frameworks like **Apache Hadoop** and **Apache Spark**.

By leveraging these languages and tools, developers and data scientists can build sophisticated models, analyze large datasets, and generate insights that drive business decisions.

Chapter 13: Debugging and Optimizing High-Level Code

Objective:

In this chapter, we'll dive into the essential skills of **debugging** and **optimizing** high-level code. Understanding how to identify and fix issues, along with improving the performance of your code, is crucial for building efficient and reliable software. We will discuss debugging tools available for popular languages like **C**, **Java**, and **Python**, and explore techniques for **profiling** and **performance tuning**. Additionally, we will go through **code optimization** practices that help improve speed and reduce memory usage. The chapter will also cover common programming pitfalls and provide practical tips on how to avoid them. To wrap it up, we'll walk through a hands-on example where we debug and optimize a **slow-running Python program**.

13.1 Introduction to Debugging and Code Optimization

Writing code is just the first step in the development process. The real challenge often comes in ensuring that code is **bug-free, efficient**, and **easy to maintain**. Debugging and optimization are critical aspects of writing high-quality code, and they require a set of skills and tools that every developer should master.

13.1.1 WHY DEBUGGING IS ESSENTIAL

Debugging is the process of identifying, isolating, and fixing problems (or **bugs**) in code. It is an essential part of development, as it ensures that the code functions as expected. Bugs can range from simple syntax errors to more complex logical errors that may be harder to detect. **Effective debugging** helps improve code quality and ensures that the software is reliable and behaves correctly under different conditions.

13.1.2 THE IMPORTANCE OF CODE OPTIMIZATION

Code optimization refers to the process of improving the performance of your program, whether it's through reducing execution time, lowering memory usage, or making the code more readable. Optimization is essential for applications that handle large datasets, run in performance-critical environments, or need to run efficiently on resource-limited systems.

There's always a trade-off between readability, maintainability, and performance. The goal of optimization is to balance these factors effectively without sacrificing the clarity of your code.

13.2 Debugging Tools for C, Java, and Python

Each programming language has its own set of tools and techniques for debugging. Whether you are working with **C**, **Java**, or **Python**, understanding how to effectively use these debugging tools is crucial for efficiently identifying and fixing issues in your code.

13.2.1 DEBUGGING IN C

C is a powerful and flexible language, but it lacks the automatic memory management found in higher-level languages, which can make debugging more challenging. However, there are several powerful tools to help debug C programs.

- **GDB (GNU Debugger)**: **GDB** is one of the most widely used debuggers for C programs. It allows you to run your program step-by-step, inspect variables, set breakpoints, and even modify variables at runtime.
  - **Basic GDB Usage**:
    - Start GDB with the program:
      `gdb ./my_program`
    - Set breakpoints: `break main`
    - Run the program: `run`
    - Step through the program: `step` or `next`
    - Print variable values: `print variable_name`
    - Exit GDB: `quit`

Example of using GDB:

```bash

gdb ./my_program
(gdb) break main
(gdb) run
(gdb) step
```

- **Valgrind**: **Valgrind** is an excellent tool for memory debugging in C. It helps identify memory leaks, uninitialized memory reads, and other memory-related errors.

```bash

valgrind --leak-check=full ./my_program
```

13.2.2 DEBUGGING IN JAVA

Java provides a robust set of debugging tools for identifying issues in your code.

- **Eclipse/IntelliJ IDEA Debuggers**: Integrated Development Environments (IDEs) like **Eclipse** and **IntelliJ IDEA** offer built-in debugging tools that allow you to set breakpoints, step through your code, and inspect variable values. These debuggers are user-friendly and ideal for developers who prefer a graphical interface.
  - **Using Eclipse Debugger**:
    - Set breakpoints by clicking the left margin next to the line number.
    - Run the program in debug mode.
    - Step through the code with buttons for "Step Into," "Step Over," and "Resume."
- **JDB (Java Debugger)**: If you prefer working in a terminal, **JDB** is a command-line debugger that comes with the JDK. It allows you to set breakpoints, inspect variables, and evaluate expressions.

```bash
jdb MyClass
> stop in MyClass.main
> run
> next
> print variableName
```

13.2.3 DEBUGGING IN PYTHON

Python's built-in debugger is called **pdb** (Python Debugger), and it is easy to use for stepping through Python code and inspecting variables.

- **Using pdb**:

- To start the debugger, insert `import pdb;` `pdb.set_trace()` in your code where you want to start debugging.
- Use `n` to step to the next line, `s` to step into a function, `c` to continue execution, and `q` to quit the debugger.

Example:

```python
import pdb
x = 10
y = 20
pdb.set_trace()   # Debugger will start here
z = x + y
print(z)
```

- You can also use **IDE-based debuggers** like those in **PyCharm** or **VSCode** for a graphical debugging experience.

13.3 Profiling and Performance Tuning Techniques

Once your code is bug-free, the next step is to optimize it for performance. Profiling is the process of measuring the performance of your program in terms of time, memory usage, and other resources. This helps identify bottlenecks and areas for improvement.

13.3.1 PROFILING IN C

In C, profiling can be done using tools like **gprof** or **Valgrind's Callgrind**.

- **gprof**: **gprof** is a profiler that analyzes the performance of your C program by tracking function call counts, execution time, and more.

  To use **gprof**:

    o Compile with –pg flag: `gcc -pg -o my_program my_program.c`
    o Run your program to generate the profiling data: `./my_program`
    o Generate the profile report: `gprof my_program gmon.out > analysis.txt`
- **Valgrind's Callgrind: Callgrind** is used for detailed cache and memory profiling. It generates reports that can be visualized with tools like **KCachegrind**.

13.3.2 PROFILING IN JAVA

Java provides several built-in tools for profiling, including **Java VisualVM** and **JProfiler**.

- **Java VisualVM: Java VisualVM** is a tool that comes with the JDK for profiling Java applications. It allows you to monitor memory usage, CPU usage, and thread activity.
    o To use Java VisualVM, launch it by typing `jvisualvm` in the terminal.
    o Attach it to a running JVM process and start profiling.
- **JProfiler: JProfiler** is a commercial tool that provides detailed insights into Java performance. It supports CPU, memory, thread, and heap analysis.

Python's **cProfile** and **timeit** modules are useful for profiling and measuring the performance of Python code.

- **cProfile**: This module allows you to track function calls and measure how long each function takes to execute.

  ```python
  python

  import cProfile
  def my_function():
      # Code to be profiled
      pass
  cProfile.run('my_function()')
  ```

- **timeit**: This module is useful for measuring the execution time of small code snippets. It is especially useful for benchmarking algorithms.

  Example:

  ```python
  python

  import timeit
  print(timeit.timeit("sum(range(100))",
  number=1000))
  ```

13.4 Code Optimization for Speed and Memory Usage

Optimizing code for **speed** and **memory usage** is essential for applications that need to handle large datasets or operate under strict performance constraints.

13.4.1 OPTIMIZING SPEED

To optimize the speed of your code, focus on the following techniques:

- **Use Efficient Algorithms**: The choice of algorithm has a significant impact on performance. For example, choosing an **O(n log n)** sorting algorithm like **merge sort** or **quick sort** is more efficient than an **O(n^2)** algorithm like **bubble sort**.
- **Avoid Redundant Computations**: Cache results of expensive computations when possible (e.g., using **memoization** or **dynamic programming** techniques).
- **Leverage Built-in Functions**: High-level languages often have optimized built-in functions (e.g., `sort()` in Python, `Arrays.sort()` in Java) that are faster than custom implementations.
- **Parallelism and Concurrency**: Use multiple threads or processes to perform tasks in parallel, especially for CPU-bound tasks.

13.4.2 OPTIMIZING MEMORY USAGE

To reduce memory consumption, follow these practices:

- **Use Memory-Efficient Data Structures**: In Python, for example, use **generators** instead of lists for large data, as they do not store the entire dataset in memory at once.
- **Avoid Memory Leaks**: In languages like C and C++, manually free memory after it is no longer needed. In languages with garbage collection, like Python and Java, ensure that references to unused objects are removed.
- **Use In-Place Modifications**: In many cases, modifying data structures **in place** (instead of creating copies) can reduce memory usage significantly.

13.5 Common Pitfalls and How to Avoid Them

Here are some common programming pitfalls and how to avoid them:

13.5.1 MEMORY LEAKS

Memory leaks occur when a program allocates memory but fails to release it when it is no longer needed. In languages like **C**, this can happen if `malloc()` is used without `free()`. In Python, memory leaks are often caused by **circular references** or lingering references to objects.

- **Solution**: Always ensure that memory is freed properly, and use tools like **Valgrind** or **Python's gc module** to detect memory leaks.

13.5.2 INFINITE LOOPS

An infinite loop occurs when a loop's exit condition is never met, causing the program to run forever.

- **Solution**: Carefully check the conditions in `while` and `for` loops to ensure that they will eventually terminate.

13.5.3 OFF-BY-ONE ERRORS

Off-by-one errors are common in loops and array indexing, where an index is incorrectly incremented or decremented, leading to incorrect results or accessing out-of-bound memory.

- **Solution**: Always double-check the range of indices in loops and array accesses, especially when iterating over data structures.

13.6 Hands-On Example: Debug and Optimize a Slow-Running Python Program

Let's walk through an example of debugging and optimizing a **slow-running Python program**. We'll start with a basic program that calculates the sum of squares of even numbers in a list, which is inefficient and slow.

STEP 1: THE IMPERATIVE VERSION (SLOW AND INEFFICIENT)

python

```python
def sum_of_squares(nums):
    result = 0
    for num in nums:
        if num % 2 == 0:
            result += num * num
    return result

nums = list(range(1, 1000000))
print(sum_of_squares(nums))
```

This code is **inefficient** because:

- It loops over the entire list and checks if each number is even.
- It performs repeated calculations, which could be optimized.

STEP 2: PROFILING THE PROGRAM

To understand why the program is slow, we'll profile it using **cProfile**.

python

```
import cProfile

cProfile.run('sum_of_squares(nums)')
```

This will output information about where time is being spent in the program, which can help us identify the bottlenecks.

STEP 3: OPTIMIZATION USING LIST COMPREHENSION AND BUILT-IN FUNCTIONS

We can optimize the program by using **list comprehension** and reducing the number of operations.

```python
python

def optimized_sum_of_squares(nums):
    return sum(x * x for x in nums if x % 2 == 0)

print(optimized_sum_of_squares(nums))
```

List comprehension is faster because it avoids the overhead of a `for` loop and leverages Python's optimized internal functions.

13.7 Conclusion

Debugging and optimization are critical skills for any software developer. Understanding how to effectively use debugging tools, profile code, and optimize performance can make a significant difference in the efficiency and quality of your applications. This chapter has covered essential tools and techniques for **debugging** in **C, Java,** and **Python**, as well as strategies for **profiling** and **optimizing** your code for speed and memory usage. By following these practices and avoiding common pitfalls, you can ensure that your code is both efficient and reliable.

Chapter 14: Testing High-Level Code

Objective:

In this chapter, we will explore the critical role of **testing** in high-level programming languages and how to ensure that your code works as expected. We'll cover the fundamentals of **unit testing**, best practices for **test-driven development (TDD)**, and how to use **mocking** and **stubbing** to isolate components during testing. We will also introduce **continuous integration** tools that automate the process of running tests. To bring these concepts to life, we'll walk through practical hands-on examples of writing and running **unit tests** in **Java** and **Python** using testing frameworks like **JUnit** and **PyTest**.

14.1 Introduction to Testing in High-Level Programming Languages

Testing is a cornerstone of **high-quality software development**. It ensures that code behaves as expected and helps identify and fix issues before they impact the end-user. In high-level programming, testing is especially important due to the complexity and scale of modern applications. Whether you're building a web application, a mobile app, or a data-processing system, ensuring that your code is thoroughly tested is crucial for maintaining reliability and robustness.

While manual testing can help uncover issues, **automated testing** is the key to improving productivity and consistency. Automated tests can be run repeatedly, ensuring that bugs are caught early in the development process and preventing regressions as new features are added.

14.2 Unit Testing in Java, Python, and C

Unit testing is a type of software testing where individual components (or **units**) of the program are tested in isolation. The goal is to ensure that each unit of code works as expected in isolation, independent of other units.

14.2.1 Unit Testing in Java

In Java, **JUnit** is the most widely used framework for writing and running unit tests. JUnit provides annotations and assertions to define test methods, run them, and check for expected outcomes.

- **Key Features of JUnit:**
  - **Annotations:** `@Test`, `@Before`, `@After`, etc., to define the lifecycle of a test.
  - **Assertions:** Methods like `assertEquals()`, `assertTrue()`, `assertNull()` to check conditions.
  - **Test Suites:** A way to group multiple test classes together and run them as a single suite.

Example of Unit Testing in Java with JUnit:

```java
import org.junit.Test;
import static org.junit.Assert.*;
```

```
public class CalculatorTest {

    @Test
    public void testAdd() {
        Calculator calc = new Calculator();
        int result = calc.add(2, 3);
        assertEquals(5, result);
    }

    @Test
    public void testSubtract() {
        Calculator calc = new Calculator();
        int result = calc.subtract(5, 3);
        assertEquals(2, result);
    }
}
```

In this example, the `CalculatorTest` class contains two test methods: `testAdd()` and `testSubtract()`. Each method creates an instance of the `Calculator` class and verifies that the methods `add()` and `subtract()` return the expected results.

14.2.2 UNIT TESTING IN PYTHON

In Python, the most commonly used framework for unit testing is **PyTest**, which is known for its simplicity and flexibility. PyTest can be used to write simple tests as well as complex ones, and it integrates seamlessly with Python's built-in `unittest` framework.

- **Key Features of PyTest**:
  - **Simple syntax**: No need for classes or boilerplate code.
  - **Fixtures**: Functions that provide setup code, such as creating database connections or preparing test data.
  - **Assertions**: PyTest uses Python's built-in `assert` statement for checking conditions.

   o **Test discovery**: Automatically discovers tests based on naming conventions (e.g., files starting with `test_`).

Example of Unit Testing in Python with PyTest:

```python
python

# calculator.py
def add(a, b):
    return a + b

def subtract(a, b):
    return a - b

# test_calculator.py
import pytest
from calculator import add, subtract

def test_add():
    assert add(2, 3) == 5

def test_subtract():
    assert subtract(5, 3) == 2
```

In this example, we define two functions, `add()` and `subtract()`, and create a test file `test_calculator.py` where we use PyTest's simple `assert` syntax to verify that the functions return the expected results.

14.2.3 UNIT TESTING IN C

Unit testing in **C** can be more challenging due to the lack of built-in frameworks. However, there are popular libraries like **CMocka** and **Unity** that provide functionality for writing and running unit tests.

- **Key Features of CMocka/Unity:**

- o **Test Assertions**: Use assertions to verify the behavior of C functions.
- o **Mocking**: Some frameworks support mocking functions to isolate units for testing.
- o **Test Suites**: Similar to Java and Python, you can group tests into suites and run them all at once.

Example of Unit Testing in C with Unity:

c

```c
#include "unity.h"

int add(int a, int b) {
    return a + b;
}

void test_add(void) {
    TEST_ASSERT_EQUAL(5, add(2, 3));
}

int main(void) {
    UNITY_BEGIN();
    RUN_TEST(test_add);
    return UNITY_END();
}
```

In this example, we use the **Unity** testing framework to test the add() function. The TEST_ASSERT_EQUAL function is used to check if the result of add(2, 3) is 5.

14.3 Test-Driven Development (TDD)

Test-Driven Development (TDD) is a software development process where tests are written before the actual code. The process follows a simple cycle known as **Red-Green-Refactor**:

1. **Red**: Write a test that fails (because the functionality isn't implemented yet).
2. **Green**: Write the minimal code necessary to pass the test.
3. **Refactor**: Clean up the code while ensuring the test still passes.

TDD helps ensure that your code is thoroughly tested and that new code doesn't introduce bugs into existing functionality.

14.3.1 BENEFITS OF TDD

- **Better Code Quality**: TDD encourages writing small, testable units of code, which leads to more maintainable and reliable software.
- **Faster Debugging**: With tests written upfront, developers can identify issues as soon as they appear.
- **Improved Design**: TDD forces developers to think about how the code will be tested, often leading to better software design.

14.3.2 TDD EXAMPLE IN JAVA

Let's take the `add()` function from earlier and write tests before the implementation.

1. **Write the test** (The test will fail initially):

    ```java
    @Test
    public void testAdd() {
        Calculator calc = new Calculator();
        assertEquals(5, calc.add(2, 3));
    }
    ```

2. **Write just enough code to pass the test:**

```java
public class Calculator {
    public int add(int a, int b) {
        return a + b;   // Minimal
implementation
    }
}
```

3. **Refactor**: After the test passes, you can improve the implementation if needed.

14.4 Mocking and Stubbing in Unit Tests

Unit tests often require isolating the code being tested from external dependencies (such as databases, APIs, or file systems). This is where **mocking** and **stubbing** come into play.

- **Mocking**: A mock object simulates the behavior of real objects in controlled ways. It is useful for testing interactions between objects.
- **Stubbing**: A stub is an object that provides predefined responses to method calls, allowing you to test code in isolation without relying on actual implementations.

14.4.1 MOCKING IN JAVA

In Java, **Mockito** is one of the most popular libraries for mocking.

Example using **Mockito**:

```java
import static org.mockito.Mockito.*;
import org.junit.Test;
```

```java
public class UserServiceTest {
    @Test
    public void testGetUserInfo() {
        UserService userService =
mock(UserService.class);

when(userService.getUserInfo(1)).thenReturn("John
Doe");

        assertEquals("John Doe",
userService.getUserInfo(1));
    }
}
```

In this example, the `UserService` is mocked, and we define a stubbed method (`getUserInfo()`) to return a specific value.

14.4.2 MOCKING IN PYTHON

In Python, **unittest.mock** is the standard library used for mocking.

Example using **unittest.mock**:

```python
python

from unittest.mock import MagicMock
import pytest

def get_user_info(user_id):
    # Simulated function that would normally make a
database call
    return "User Info"

def test_get_user_info():
    mock_func = MagicMock(return_value="John Doe")
    result = mock_func(1)
    assert result == "John Doe"
```

Here, we create a mock function that returns `"John Doe"` when called.

14.5 Continuous Integration Tools

Continuous Integration (CI) is the practice of automatically testing and building code whenever changes are made. CI ensures that new code integrates smoothly with the existing codebase and that no tests fail.

- **Jenkins**: One of the most popular open-source CI tools that can automate the building, testing, and deployment of applications.
- **CircleCI**: Another cloud-based CI service that integrates with GitHub and Bitbucket.
- **Travis CI**: Provides continuous integration and deployment for GitHub projects.
- **GitLab CI**: GitLab's built-in CI tool that allows automation directly within GitLab repositories.

Example Workflow:

1. **Push Code to Repository**: Developers push their code to a shared repository (e.g., GitHub, GitLab).
2. **Automated Test Run**: The CI tool automatically triggers the build and test process.
3. **Feedback**: The results of the test are sent to developers. If any test fails, the developers are notified, and they can fix the issue before pushing new code.

14.6 Hands-On Example: Write and Run Unit Tests for a Java or Python Application Using JUnit or PyTest

Let's walk through an example where we write unit tests for a simple **Python** or **Java** application using **PyTest** or **JUnit**.

HANDS-ON EXAMPLE IN PYTHON USING PYTEST

1. **Write the Application Code:**

   python

   ```python
   def add(a, b):
       return a + b

   def subtract(a, b):
       return a - b
   ```

2. **Write Unit Tests:**

   python

   ```python
   import pytest
   from calculator import add, subtract

   def test_add():
       assert add(2, 3) == 5

   def test_subtract():
       assert subtract(5, 3) == 2
   ```

3. **Run the Tests:**

   bash

   ```bash
   pytest test_calculator.py
   ```

1. **Write the Application Code:**

```java
public class Calculator {
    public int add(int a, int b) {
        return a + b;
    }

    public int subtract(int a, int b) {
        return a - b;
    }
}
```

2. **Write Unit Tests:**

```java
import static org.junit.Assert.*;
import org.junit.Test;

public class CalculatorTest {

    @Test
    public void testAdd() {
        Calculator calc = new Calculator();
        assertEquals(5, calc.add(2, 3));
    }

    @Test
    public void testSubtract() {
        Calculator calc = new Calculator();
        assertEquals(2, calc.subtract(5, 3));
    }
}
```

3. **Run the Tests:** Use your IDE (Eclipse, IntelliJ) or command line to run the tests and verify that everything works as expected.

14.7 Conclusion

Testing is a critical part of software development that ensures reliability, correctness, and maintainability. By mastering **unit testing, test-driven development (TDD),** and **mocking** and **stubbing** techniques, developers can write more robust applications and avoid common pitfalls. Using **CI tools** allows teams to automate testing and catch issues early in the development process.

By the end of this chapter, you should have a solid understanding of how to implement testing best practices in both **Java** and **Python**, and how to use modern tools and frameworks to make the testing process more efficient and effective.

Chapter 15: The Future of High-Level Programming Languages

Objective:

In this chapter, we will look ahead to the future of **high-level programming languages**. As technology continues to advance, new trends and innovations are shaping the way we write code. From **quantum programming** to the integration of **AI and machine learning** in programming languages, there are exciting developments on the horizon. We'll also explore how new languages are being designed to be more **efficient** and **expressive** and discuss the future of **microservices, serverless computing**, and **cloud-native applications**. To conclude the chapter, we'll dive into a **hands-on example** where we build a small **AI-powered application** using **Python** and **TensorFlow**, demonstrating how high-level languages are evolving to integrate with modern technologies.

15.1 Introduction to the Future of High-Level Programming Languages

The landscape of software development has been rapidly evolving, and high-level programming languages have played a crucial role in making this possible. As technology progresses, there are emerging trends and innovations that promise to revolutionize the way we write and interact with code. In this chapter, we'll explore some of the most exciting directions in which high-level languages are headed.

15.1.1 The Role of High-Level Languages in the Modern Software Ecosystem

High-level programming languages have become indispensable for building scalable, maintainable, and complex software applications. These languages, with their **abstraction layers,** make it easier for developers to focus on solving business problems rather than worrying about low-level hardware details.

In the coming years, high-level languages will continue to evolve to address the growing demands for **performance, efficiency, scalability,** and **expressiveness.** As the world becomes more data-driven and interconnected, the need for languages that can seamlessly integrate with **AI, cloud computing,** and **quantum technologies** will be more important than ever.

15.2 The Rise of Quantum Programming Languages

One of the most exciting developments on the horizon is the rise of **quantum programming languages.** Quantum computing, which leverages the principles of quantum mechanics to perform calculations, has the potential to solve problems that are currently intractable for classical computers.

15.2.1 What is Quantum Computing?

Quantum computing relies on quantum bits, or **qubits,** which can exist in multiple states simultaneously (superposition), unlike classical bits that are either 0 or 1. Quantum computers can perform complex calculations at a much faster rate than classical computers by exploiting these quantum properties.

For instance, while classical computers struggle with tasks like **factorizing large numbers** or simulating quantum systems, quantum computers can potentially solve these tasks in polynomial time, making them incredibly powerful for certain applications, including cryptography, drug discovery, and optimization problems.

15.2.2 QUANTUM PROGRAMMING LANGUAGES

As quantum computing becomes more practical, the need for specialized quantum programming languages is growing. These languages are designed to express quantum algorithms and enable developers to harness the power of quantum computers. Some of the prominent quantum programming languages include:

- **Qiskit**: Developed by IBM, Qiskit is an open-source quantum programming framework built on Python. It allows developers to create quantum circuits and run quantum algorithms on simulators or actual quantum hardware.
- **Quipper**: A high-level functional programming language designed specifically for quantum computing. Quipper allows developers to design quantum algorithms in a way that resembles classical functional programming.
- **Microsoft Q#**: A language developed by Microsoft for quantum programming. Q# is used to write quantum algorithms, and it integrates with the **Quantum Development Kit** (QDK) to simulate and run quantum programs on real quantum hardware.

15.2.3 THE FUTURE OF QUANTUM PROGRAMMING

In the near future, we will likely see more high-level quantum programming languages emerge that simplify the complexities of quantum computing. These languages will focus on making quantum computing more accessible to developers from classical programming backgrounds, enabling them to build quantum algorithms without needing to be experts in quantum mechanics.

Quantum programming will eventually become a critical part of high-level programming, especially as we move toward **hybrid systems** that combine classical and quantum computing for optimal performance.

15.3 The Integration of AI and Machine Learning in Programming Languages

Artificial Intelligence (AI) and Machine Learning (ML) are becoming an integral part of modern software applications. As the demand for intelligent systems grows, programming languages are evolving to provide better tools and abstractions for AI and ML.

15.3.1 AI-DRIVEN DEVELOPMENT TOOLS

The integration of AI into programming languages is enhancing the developer experience. AI-powered tools can assist developers by automatically generating code, detecting bugs, suggesting improvements, and even writing documentation. These tools are already improving the speed and quality of software development.

For example, tools like **GitHub Copilot**, powered by OpenAI's GPT-3, provide real-time code suggestions based on context, making it easier for developers to write code more efficiently.

15.3.2 MACHINE LEARNING FRAMEWORKS

In the context of programming languages, **machine learning frameworks** like **TensorFlow**, **PyTorch**, and **Scikit-learn** are already part of the software development ecosystem. These frameworks allow developers to build, train, and deploy machine learning models with minimal effort.

- **TensorFlow**: A popular open-source framework developed by Google, TensorFlow simplifies the development of deep learning models, especially for tasks like image recognition, natural language processing, and reinforcement learning.
- **PyTorch**: Another widely used deep learning framework, developed by Facebook. PyTorch is favored for its dynamic computation graph, making it easier to work with complex models and experiments.
- **Scikit-learn**: A more general-purpose machine learning framework, Scikit-learn is ideal for tasks like classification, regression, and clustering. It provides a simple interface to apply machine learning algorithms to structured data.

15.3.3 MACHINE LEARNING IN HIGH-LEVEL PROGRAMMING LANGUAGES

As machine learning continues to be integrated into programming languages, we will see even greater support for AI-powered applications. High-level languages like **Python** have become synonymous with machine learning due to the ease of use, vast ecosystem of libraries, and high-level abstractions.

The future will see more programming languages built with **machine learning** in mind, offering even higher-level abstractions to make it easier to create intelligent applications. Newer languages may also natively support **AI models**, allowing developers to seamlessly incorporate machine learning models into their applications without relying on external libraries.

15.4 How New Languages Are Designed to Be More Efficient and Expressive

The development of new programming languages is often driven by the need for **efficiency** and **expressiveness**. High-level languages are constantly evolving to be more powerful while remaining easy to use. This trend will continue as developers face the growing demands for software that is both **high-performance** and **easy to maintain**.

15.4.1 EFFICIENCY IN HIGH-LEVEL PROGRAMMING LANGUAGES

Efficiency is one of the key goals for new programming languages. Modern applications require faster processing speeds, more responsive user interfaces, and the ability to handle larger datasets. New languages are being designed to optimize performance while maintaining high-level abstractions.

- **Memory Management**: Many modern languages are addressing memory management issues by incorporating features like automatic garbage collection or fine-tuned memory allocation strategies.
- **Concurrency and Parallelism**: New languages are being designed with built-in support for **concurrency** and **parallelism**, allowing developers to write multi-threaded programs more easily and efficiently. Languages like **Go** and **Rust** are built with concurrency in mind, providing efficient ways to handle concurrent tasks.

Programming languages must be expressive, allowing developers to write clean, concise, and maintainable code. **Functional programming, object-oriented programming**, and **declarative programming** paradigms are being integrated into new languages to increase their expressiveness and versatility.

For example:

- **Rust** offers a unique approach to ownership and borrowing, enabling developers to write safe and efficient code with fewer bugs.
- **Swift** and **Kotlin** provide modern syntax and powerful features like **null safety, type inference**, and **closures**, making them more expressive compared to older languages like **Objective-C** or **Java**.

These new languages are designed to minimize boilerplate code and provide powerful abstractions that allow developers to focus more on solving business problems than managing the language's intricacies.

15.5 The Future of Microservices, Serverless, and Cloud-Native Applications

As the demand for scalable and flexible applications grows, the **microservices architecture** and **serverless computing** are becoming increasingly popular. These approaches enable developers to build distributed systems that are more modular, scalable, and resilient.

15.5.1 MICROSERVICES AND HIGH-LEVEL PROGRAMMING LANGUAGES

Microservices are small, independently deployable services that each handle a specific function of the application. High-level languages like **Java, Python**, and **Go** have emerged as the go-to tools for building microservices due to their ability to quickly prototype and scale applications.

The future will see **microservices** becoming even more prevalent, with more languages and frameworks being designed to support this architectural style. Tools like **Docker** and **Kubernetes** are already simplifying the deployment and management of microservices.

15.5.2 SERVERLESS COMPUTING

Serverless computing is a model where developers can build and run applications without managing infrastructure. In serverless computing, cloud providers automatically manage the servers and scaling. Popular serverless platforms include **AWS Lambda, Google Cloud Functions**, and **Azure Functions**.

High-level languages like **JavaScript, Python**, and **Go** are commonly used in serverless environments due to their quick startup times and efficient memory management.

15.5.3 CLOUD-NATIVE APPLICATIONS

Cloud-native applications are built and deployed to run in the cloud, taking advantage of cloud services like **elastic scaling, distributed databases,** and **containerization**. High-level languages are increasingly being designed to integrate seamlessly with cloud-native ecosystems, simplifying the development of scalable, distributed systems.

15.6 Hands-On Example: Build a Small AI-Powered Application Using Python and TensorFlow

Now, let's bring all the concepts together and create a simple **AI-powered application** using **Python** and **TensorFlow**. We'll build a model that predicts **housing prices** based on various input features such as the number of rooms, square footage, and location.

STEP 1: IMPORT REQUIRED LIBRARIES

python

```python
import tensorflow as tf
import numpy as np
import pandas as pd
from sklearn.model_selection import train_test_split
from sklearn.preprocessing import StandardScaler
```

STEP 2: LOAD AND PREPARE DATA

For this example, let's assume we have a dataset with features like **size**, **location**, and **number of rooms**.

python

```python
# Load dataset (For demonstration, we use synthetic
data)
data = pd.read_csv('housing_data.csv')

# Split into features and target
X = data.drop('price', axis=1)  # Features
```

```python
y = data['price']  # Target variable (housing prices)

# Split into training and testing sets
X_train, X_test, y_train, y_test =
train_test_split(X, y, test_size=0.2,
random_state=42)

# Standardize the features
scaler = StandardScaler()
X_train = scaler.fit_transform(X_train)
X_test = scaler.transform(X_test)
```

STEP 3: BUILD THE NEURAL NETWORK MODEL

python

```python
model = tf.keras.Sequential([
    tf.keras.layers.Dense(64, activation='relu',
input_shape=(X_train.shape[1],)),
    tf.keras.layers.Dense(32, activation='relu'),
    tf.keras.layers.Dense(1)  # Output layer for
regression (single value output)
])

model.compile(optimizer='adam',
loss='mean_squared_error')
```

STEP 4: TRAIN THE MODEL

python

```python
history = model.fit(X_train, y_train, epochs=100,
validation_data=(X_test, y_test))
```

STEP 5: EVALUATE AND PREDICT

python

```python
# Evaluate the model
loss = model.evaluate(X_test, y_test)
print(f'Loss: {loss}')
```

```
# Predict housing prices
predictions = model.predict(X_test)
```

15.7 Conclusion

The future of high-level programming languages is incredibly exciting. From **quantum computing** to **AI integration** and the development of more **expressive** and **efficient languages**, the landscape is evolving rapidly. High-level languages like **Python**, **Java**, and **JavaScript** are adapting to these trends, allowing developers to build powerful, scalable, and intelligent applications with ease.

As we move into an era of **cloud-native applications**, **microservices**, and **serverless computing**, the role of high-level languages will only continue to grow. By staying informed about the latest trends and continuously improving your skills in these areas, you will be well-equipped to take on the challenges of the future.

Appendix: Key Resources and Further Reading

Objective:

In this appendix, we provide a comprehensive collection of resources for readers who wish to deepen their understanding of **high-level programming languages**. Whether you are looking to expand your knowledge through **books, online courses**, or **communities**, or seeking **tools** and **IDEs** to improve your coding workflow, this guide has something for everyone. Additionally, we'll highlight **advanced topics** that you can explore to take your programming expertise to the next level. The goal is to equip you with the resources you need to continue your journey in the world of high-level programming languages and stay up-to-date with the latest developments.

---

1. Recommended Books

Books remain one of the best ways to gain in-depth knowledge and learn concepts in high-level programming languages. Here's a curated list of **recommended books** that will guide you through the fundamentals, advanced topics, and best practices.

1.1. FOR BEGINNERS AND INTERMEDIATE LEARNERS

1. **"Python Crash Course" by Eric Matthes**
   - Overview: This book is perfect for beginners looking to learn Python. It covers basic concepts and moves

into practical examples, such as building web applications and working with data.

- o **Why It's Useful**: If you're just starting with Python, this book offers a hands-on approach to learning. It's suitable for individuals looking to build projects while mastering the language.

2. **"Head First Java" by Kathy Sierra and Bert Bates**
   - o **Overview**: A beginner-friendly book that teaches Java through visually rich, interactive learning techniques. It breaks down complex topics into digestible chunks.
   - o **Why It's Useful**: Head First Java is ideal for those new to programming or Java. The engaging format helps keep learners motivated.

3. **"JavaScript: The Good Parts" by Douglas Crockford**
   - o **Overview**: This book focuses on the best features of JavaScript, encouraging developers to adopt a simpler, cleaner approach to the language.
   - o **Why It's Useful**: For JavaScript developers who want to master the core concepts of the language without getting bogged down by unnecessary complexity, this book offers a concise, practical perspective.

4. **"The Pragmatic Programmer: Your Journey to Mastery" by Andrew Hunt and David Thomas**
   - o **Overview**: While not specific to one language, this book is a comprehensive guide for developers looking to improve their coding practices, regardless of the programming language they use.
   - o **Why It's Useful**: It provides invaluable insight into best practices for coding, debugging, and thinking like a professional developer.

1.2. ADVANCED LEARNERS AND EXPERTS

1. **"Structure and Interpretation of Computer Programs" by Harold Abelson, Gerald Jay Sussman**

- Overview: Often referred to as SICP, this book is a classic in the field of computer science. It covers foundational topics in programming, such as recursion, abstraction, and language design, with a focus on Scheme (a dialect of Lisp).
- Why It's Useful: It's a deep dive into the concepts behind programming languages, algorithms, and computation. This book is ideal for learners who want to explore language design and computational theory.

2. **"Design Patterns: Elements of Reusable Object-Oriented Software" by Erich Gamma, Richard Helm, Ralph Johnson, John Vlissides**
   - Overview: Known as the "Gang of Four" book, this is the go-to reference for learning **design patterns** in object-oriented software development.
   - Why It's Useful: This book is crucial for those who want to understand how to build reusable, maintainable, and scalable systems in object-oriented languages like Java and Python.

3. **"Programming Pearls" by Jon Bentley**
   - Overview: This book is a collection of essays that discuss how to write clean, efficient, and optimized code, touching on algorithms, data structures, and practical coding problems.
   - Why It's Useful: It's a great read for advanced programmers who are looking to refine their problem-solving skills and improve the efficiency of their solutions.

4. **"Introduction to Algorithms" by Thomas H. Cormen, Charles E. Leiserson, Ronald L. Rivest, Clifford Stein**
   - Overview: Commonly referred to as **CLRS**, this book provides a comprehensive introduction to algorithms, covering topics like sorting, dynamic programming, graph algorithms, and more.

- o **Why It's Useful**: Ideal for those looking to deepen their understanding of algorithms and their applications in programming.

---

2. Online Courses and Tutorials

Online courses have become one of the most accessible and effective ways to learn programming. Below are some of the best **online courses** and **tutorials** that offer structured learning paths for both beginners and advanced learners.

2.1. FOR BEGINNERS AND INTERMEDIATE LEARNERS

1. **Coursera: "Python for Everybody" by the University of Michigan**
   - o **Overview**: This is a beginner-friendly course that teaches Python programming from scratch. It covers topics like basic syntax, data structures, and web scraping.
   - o **Why It's Useful**: It's well-structured and includes practical assignments that will help you develop real-world Python skills.
2. **Udemy: "The Complete Java Developer Course" by Tim Buchalka**
   - o **Overview**: A comprehensive course for those who want to learn Java. It covers everything from the basics to advanced topics like multi-threading and data structures.
   - o **Why It's Useful**: Udemy courses are highly practical, with a focus on building projects and coding challenges that reinforce learning.
3. **Codecademy: "Learn JavaScript"**

- o **Overview**: A hands-on, interactive course that covers JavaScript fundamentals, including DOM manipulation, asynchronous programming, and modern JavaScript syntax.
- o **Why It's Useful**: Codecademy's interactive learning platform allows learners to write code in the browser and receive instant feedback.
4. **freeCodeCamp: Full Stack Developer Certification**
   - o **Overview**: freeCodeCamp offers a self-paced learning platform where you can learn web development by building projects. The course includes **HTML**, **CSS**, **JavaScript**, and backend technologies like **Node.js**.
   - o **Why It's Useful**: It's an excellent, completely free resource for those who want to become full-stack developers.

2.2. FOR ADVANCED LEARNERS

1. **Coursera: "Machine Learning" by Andrew Ng (Stanford University)**
   - o **Overview**: This is one of the most popular machine learning courses online. It covers supervised learning, unsupervised learning, and best practices for implementing machine learning algorithms.
   - o **Why It's Useful**: Taught by Andrew Ng, one of the leading figures in AI, this course offers a solid foundation for learning machine learning.
2. **Udacity: "Data Engineering Nanodegree"**
   - o **Overview**: This program covers everything from data modeling and ETL processes to cloud computing and advanced data engineering concepts.
   - o **Why It's Useful**: Ideal for learners interested in big data, cloud architecture, and building scalable data pipelines.

3. **edX: "The Software Development Lifecycle" by UC Berkeley**
   - o **Overview**: This advanced course dives deep into the entire software development lifecycle, from requirements gathering to deployment and maintenance.
   - o **Why It's Useful**: It's perfect for developers who want to understand the bigger picture of how software projects are developed and maintained over time.

3. Communities and Forums

Being part of a **developer community** is one of the best ways to stay updated with the latest trends, ask questions, and learn from others' experiences. Here are some of the most popular programming communities.

3.1. FOR GENERAL PROGRAMMING

1. **Stack Overflow**
   - o **Overview**: Stack Overflow is a popular Q&A platform where developers can ask technical questions and get answers from the community.
   - o **Why It's Useful**: It's an invaluable resource for finding solutions to coding problems and learning from experienced developers.
2. **GitHub**
   - o **Overview**: GitHub is a code hosting platform that also serves as a social network for developers. It's home to millions of open-source projects and provides collaboration tools like version control and pull requests.

- o **Why It's Useful**: GitHub is a great place to find open-source code, collaborate with other developers, and contribute to large projects.
3. **Reddit (r/learnprogramming, r/programming, r/coding)**
   - o **Overview**: Subreddits like **r/learnprogramming** and **r/coding** are vibrant communities where programmers share tips, tutorials, and discuss coding challenges.
   - o **Why It's Useful**: Reddit is a great place to engage in discussions, ask for help, and get recommendations for tools, libraries, and best practices.

3.2. FOR PYTHON

1. **Python.org Community**
   - o **Overview**: The official Python community website features a wealth of resources, including mailing lists, forums, and events like PyCon.
   - o **Why It's Useful**: It's the best place to connect with Python enthusiasts, ask questions, and stay informed about Python-related events.
2. **Real Python**
   - o **Overview**: Real Python offers tutorials, articles, and video lessons on various Python topics, including web development, data science, and automation.
   - o **Why It's Useful**: It's a comprehensive resource for both beginners and advanced Python programmers looking to improve their skills.

3.3. FOR JAVA

1. **Stack Overflow (Java section)**
   - o **Overview**: Stack Overflow has a dedicated section for Java where developers can ask language-specific questions and get expert advice.

- o **Why It's Useful**: The Java community on Stack Overflow is large and active, offering quick solutions to almost any problem you might encounter in Java development.
2. **Java Reddit Community (r/java)**
   - o **Overview**: A subreddit focused entirely on **Java** programming. The community discusses new features, tools, frameworks, and practices related to Java.
   - o **Why It's Useful**: It's a great place for both Java beginners and experts to share experiences, ask questions, and keep up with the latest Java developments.

---

4. Tools and IDEs for Programming

Choosing the right **Integrated Development Environment (IDE)** or **tools** can significantly enhance your productivity as a developer. Here are some essential IDEs and tools used by programmers in various high-level languages.

4.1. FOR PYTHON

1. **PyCharm**
   - o **Overview**: PyCharm is one of the most popular Python IDEs, offering features like code completion, error checking, debugging, and integration with version control systems.
   - o **Why It's Useful**: It provides a rich set of tools to make Python development faster and more efficient.
2. **VSCode (Visual Studio Code)**
   - o **Overview**: VSCode is a lightweight, open-source editor that supports Python and many other

languages through extensions. It offers debugging, Git integration, and a robust extension marketplace.
- ○ **Why It's Useful**: It's customizable and can be tailored to your workflow, making it a popular choice for Python developers.

1. **IntelliJ IDEA**
   - ○ **Overview**: IntelliJ IDEA is a powerful IDE for Java development that offers features like intelligent code completion, refactoring, and integrated testing tools.
   - ○ **Why It's Useful**: It's especially good for enterprise-level Java applications, supporting a variety of frameworks and technologies.
2. **Eclipse**
   - ○ **Overview**: Eclipse is a free, open-source IDE widely used in the Java community. It's highly extensible and supports a wide range of plugins for different programming tasks.
   - ○ **Why It's Useful**: Eclipse is ideal for large Java projects, offering excellent integration with build systems like Maven and Gradle.

4.3. FOR JAVASCRIPT/NODE.JS

1. **WebStorm**
   - ○ **Overview**: WebStorm is an IDE specifically designed for JavaScript and Node.js development. It supports modern frameworks like **React**, **Vue**, and **Angular**.
   - ○ **Why It's Useful**: It provides a rich environment for building JavaScript applications with features like debugging, code analysis, and version control.
2. **VSCode (Visual Studio Code)**
   - ○ **Overview**: As mentioned earlier, VSCode is also an excellent choice for JavaScript and Node.js

development. It supports multiple extensions for enhancing JavaScript productivity.

5. Advanced Topics to Explore

For those looking to go beyond the basics, here are some advanced topics you can explore to deepen your understanding of high-level programming languages and become an even more effective developer.

5.1. COMPILERS

Understanding how **compilers** work is crucial for developers interested in language design and optimization. Learning about lexical analysis, parsing, and code generation will give you insights into how high-level languages are translated into machine code.

5.2. ADVANCED ALGORITHMS

Learning advanced algorithms is key to solving complex problems efficiently. Topics such as **graph algorithms, dynamic programming**, and **greedy algorithms** are essential for tackling challenges in fields like AI, data science, and optimization.

5.3. LANGUAGE DESIGN

As programming languages evolve, new paradigms and features emerge. **Functional programming, concurrency models**, and **type systems** are just a few areas to explore if you want to understand how programming languages are designed and improved.

Conclusion

The resources outlined in this appendix are designed to help you further your understanding of **high-level programming languages**. Whether you're just starting out or looking to deepen your expertise, there are countless resources available to support your learning journey. From books and courses to communities and tools, these resources will provide you with the knowledge and skills needed to stay ahead in the ever-evolving world of software development.

By exploring **advanced topics** like **compilers**, **language design**, and **algorithms**, you can position yourself to tackle complex problems and contribute to the development of the next generation of high-level programming languages.